Introduct

The Heart of Wales Railway links Sh
the way, passes through some of Wales' n
as being a spectacular journey, the line provid _____ walking
country, and gives you the opportunity to reach the start of each route without
the use of a car. From Shrewsbury in the north to the line's southern terminus
at Swansea these walks provide a wide range of opportunities, ranging from
town and riverside explorations to more adventurous excursions into the
mountains.

Any of these walks can be undertaken by a reasonably fit person, with
only one being more than moderately challenging. Walking boots or strong
shoes are recommended for all of them, and *please* keep in mind that this is
sheep farming country – *dogs must be kept on a lead at all times.*

The location of each walk and its station starting point is shown on the
back cover, and a summary and the length of each is given on a special chart
on the inside back cover. An *estimated* duration is also given for each walk,
but for those who enjoy fine views and like to linger over them, or to explore
the attractions visited, it is best to allow longer. If you are travelling by rail, it
is *essential* that you check the timetable, to *ensure* you have allowed sufficient
time to meet the train for your return journey. For train timetable enquiries
and tickets ring 08457 484950 or visit www.arrivatrainswales.co.uk. You can
also buy tickets on the train. Llandrindod Wells is the only staffed station
between Shrewsbury and Llanelli. Visit: www.heart-of-wales.co.uk for general
information.

Each walk has a map and description which enables the route to be followed without further help, but always take account of the weather and dress
accordingly, especially if you are exploring the higher routes.

A weather forecast for the area crossed by the line can be obtained at
www.metoffice.gov.uk or ukweather.com.

Please respect local traditions, and always take special care of the envi-
ronment, so that all those who wish to enjoy the great charm and beauty of
The Heart of Wales Line, and the countryside it passes through, may continue
to do so.

This guide would not exist without the enthusiastic support of the
Heart of Wales Line Travellers Association, especially David Edwards, Roger
Baldwin, Peter Davies, Martin Loake and all the other members who have
assisted. Special thanks are also extended to the Heart of Wales Line Forum,
who got the project 'off the ground'.

Enjoy your walking!

WALK I

DARWIN'S HOME TOWN

DESCRIPTION This walk introduces locations around Shrewsbury associated with the young Charles Darwin, the naturalist who shook the scientific world with his theory of evolution. The walk links into the Darwin town trail and leading to his birthplace, the Mount near to the River Severn. 3 miles, allow 2 hours.

START Shrewsbury Station SO495128.

I From the main entrance of Shrewsbury Railway Station walk ahead to Castle Gates. Turn left and as the road climbs go left up steps along a pathway known as the Dana. *Take a look across the road to Shrewsbury Library, at one time Dr Butler's school which the young Darwin attended. He was evidently not that interested in his school work; the school was something of a turn off. However, the handsome statue outside reflects the civic pride of the town in Darwin; it was erected in 1897. The Dana skirts the walls of Shrewsbury Castle and crosses over the railway station to reach a road by Shrewsbury gaol. Note the bust of John Howard, penal reformer above the entrance to the prison as you pass by.* Go right and follow the road to a corner where you go down steps to a riverside path (shared with bikes) by the Severn. Turn right and continue until you reach the English bridge. Climb steps, before the bridge, to Wyle Cop.

2 Turn right into Wyle Cop and keep ahead. Cross the road just before the Lion Hotel. *This old staging post inn is where Darwin caught a coach to London to seek a place on HMS Beagle.* Go left along Barracks Passage to Belmont Bank, and don't forget to look back at the Lion on the Lion Hotel; it's a superb sculpture and what a tail. Turn right at the top into Belmont then first left into Princess Street. Go right along Golden Cross Passage into High Street and left again – *to pass by the Unitarian church where the Darwin family worshipped before his mother died when he was only eight.* Continue to

the Square and turn left to pass the old Market Hall to turn right into Market Street by the Music Hall and then go first left into Swan Hill through to Murivance.

Drinkwater S
⑤ Mount House
Frankwell
Hermi
Wal

3 Go right – *to reach St Chad's church where Charles Darwin was christened soon after his birth in 1809; the circular design is very unusual. It is known for its Friday lunchtime concerts in the round, so time the walk to suit.* Just beyond St Chad's turn right into Claremont to walk down to Bellstone. Go right here to the entrance of Morris Hall Yard on the right. Proceed through the gates into the courtyard. *Have a look at the granite Bellstone, thought to have been brought here during the last Ice Age. It was an inspiration to Darwin to study geology.* Go back to the main street, cross it and walk up Claremont Street to pass by Darwin Gate on the right. However, keep left down the Mardol to reach Mardol Quay. Turn left to the pedestrian crossing and walk ahead over Welsh Bridge. *On the right is the Quantum Leap sculpture, a superb piece of art to commemorate Darwin's bi-centenary in 2009.*

4 As the road bends left go right by Theatre Severn and turn left into Whitehorse Passage which leads to Mount Street. Turn left into St George's Street and across into Hermitage Walk. Pass by a little community garden on the left, then continue on Frankwell where the path runs above the road to reach the gateway to Mount House – *where Darwin was born. Unfortunately, it is not open to the public but you can walk up the drive to take a photograph of this charming building, which dates from the 1790s.*

5 Retrace your steps along Hermitage Walk to Drinkwater Street. Turn left and at the end go right along a path, Darwin's Walk, between gardens and the river. It reaches a water meadow. Keep half right alongside the scant remains of a medieval navigation to re-join the riverside path. Continue to the Frankwell footbridge. Cross this and descend to Smithfield Road. Go right. Pass by the bus

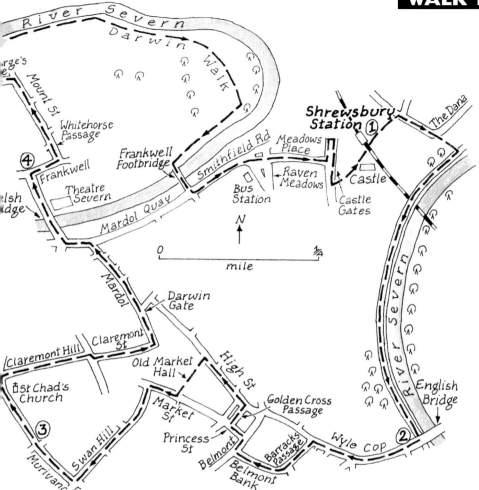

station, cross Raven Meadows and walk up Meadows Place to Castle Gates. Go left to the pedestrian crossing to the station forecourt. *Of the many cafés in Shrewsbury the Shrewsbury Coffee House on the left is one of the best, and well situated for the railway station.*

Charles Darwin was born into a family which took great interest in botany and natural history but his focus on the natural world. Thus, despite his father's reluctance it is no surprise that Darwin managed to secure a position on the second voyage of HMS Beagle in 1831. The exploration and voyage of different continents took five years thus allowing him to make extensive studies of the natural world especially in South America. On his return in 1836 he reported the findings of his studies but it was not until 1859 that he unveiled his theory of evolution. This theory revolutionised scientific thinking in that it argued that species had evolved from a common base by a process of natural selection over the centuries. This countered the widely held view of the scientific community that all species were created at one moment in time and had remained thus since. The debate still continues but Darwin's imprint on scientific thinking is stronger than ever.

WALK 2

THE LITTLE SWITZERLAND OF SHROPSHIRE

DESCRIPTION This short walk leads through the once famous Midlands spa town of Church Stretton which was so popular in earlier decades that it was dubbed as the Little Switzerland of Shropshire. The walk follows Sandford Avenue to Rectory wood and onward to Carding Mill Valley, one of the loveliest batches found in the Long Mynd. 2½ miles, allow 2 hours.
START Church Stretton Station SO456936.

I From the northbound platform of Church Stretton Railway Station, walk up the station entrance to the main street, Sandford Avenue; it is lined on the right with lime trees. *The street is named after the Reverend Holland Sandford, who was keen to plant trees throughout the town in the 19thC (to good effect).* At the top of the street go LEFT into High Street and into the Square. Turn RIGHT here along Churchway to pass the church of St Laurence on the LEFT. *By the north door of the church is a sheela-na-gig, a Saxon carving of a fertility symbol.* Cross Church Street, go ahead along a drive, and through a gate into a meadow.

2 Continue ahead and climb steps into Rectory Wood. Turn RIGHT here and follow the path through the wood to come alongside the Town Brook and restored Ice House by a pool. Continue on the main path up the valley by the stream to reach open countryside. Turn RIGHT here for Burway Road where you'll see a gateway and cattle grid to your right. Cross the road and keep ahead to walk into Carding Mill Valley; *the views of the valley beneath are exceptional.* The path descends to the road in the valley. Continue ahead and the National Trust Pavilion – *where homemade cake and tea/coffee is (almost) obligatory –* is to be found on the left. It is possible to walk up the valley if you prefer a longer walk but you will need to retrace your steps to the Pavilion afterwards.

3 From the Pavilion, turn RIGHT to walk alongside the stream and road back down the valley to leave the National Trust property. On reaching the houses look for a path between hedges on the RIGHT. This leads to Longhills Road which is much quieter than Carding Mill Valley. Go LEFT along the road back to a junction with the Burway Road. Turn LEFT and cross High Street to return to Sandford Avenue. This leads back to the railway station, which has an award winning garden.

Church Stretton was the first 'Walkers Are Welcome' town to be set up in the Midlands and there are excellent walks to the west across the Long Mynd or eastwards over Caradoc and Lawley for those seeking a longer, more strenuous ramble. If you are feeling less energetic or have younger children with you this walk is ideal, for you can view the grandeur of the surrounding countryside without the hard climbs. Whilst there are rough surfaces and some steps this is just about possible with a buggy in drier weather but not by wheelchair.

The town itself is worth exploration as it grew as a spa resort in the late decades of the 19thC up until the Edwardian era, when development plans came to an end. Mineral water is still pumped at Stretton Hills which was established in 1883. The Long Mynd Hotel is also a long standing survivor from the spa era. It was built as a hydro but plans to pump water from an aquifer in the Shropshire Hills failed and at one stage water was brought from Llandrindod Wells by train in times of shortage! The hotel, however, is still going strong and welcomes walkers.

Carding Mill Valley is one of the loveliest batches (steep sided valleys) in the Long Mynd and in the very heart of the valley is the Pavilion (with shop and tea room), dating from the 1920s and now in the ownership of the National Trust It is heated by a 50kw log boiler using coppiced wood from Wenlock Edge. There are also plans to establish a water turbine on the fast flowing streams flowing into the valley, so the

(possible extension up valley)

N.T. Pavilion ③

Longhills Road

Carding Mill Valley

Burway G Road

N

0 ¼ mile

Town Brook

Rectory Wood

②

church

High St

Sandford Ave

Church Stretton Station ①

Trust is really becoming self sufficient at this site. It is best to visit on a quiet day, as on high days and holidays the valley suffers from an endless stream of cars, and sadly the tranquillity and beauty of the place is lost at these times.

WALKERS ARE WELCOME

CHURCH STRETTON

Church Stretton

WALK 3

A WALK BACK IN TIME

DESCRIPTION This station-to-station walk meanders through undulating countryside to the Acton Scott Historic Working Farm, which splendidly recreates farming life as it was at the turn of the century. The whole route is about 8½ miles long, and will take approximately 5 hours (NOT including a visit to Acton Scott).
START Craven Arms SO432830 or Church Stretton SO445935.

I Leave Craven Arms Station from the southbound platform, walk to the main road and turn LEFT. When you reach the speed derestriction road signs, turn RIGHT along the signed path by the horse trough. Cross the footbridge and go through the kissing gate to the right. Follow the path across a field, pass through another kissing gate and turn RIGHT. Pass the 'School House' on your left and immediately turn LEFT through a stile. Walk with the hedge on your left, cross a stile and continue. Go through a gate and continue to walk ahead, now with an old hedge on your right. Continue ahead when a fence joins your route from the left. Cross a double stile and follow the path through trees, with the river below you on the left. Cross a stile into a field and continue ahead walking around trees on the left. Continue ahead, then cross a stile by a gate on the left, to follow a track under trees.

2 Pass Berrymill Cottage, go through a gate and carry on AHEAD, with a fence on your left. Go through a gateway and continue on to a stile. Cross this and walk ahead. Step across a footbridge then turn LEFT to cross another footbridge with stiles. Cross this and turn RIGHT. Cross a stile beside a gate and continue with a fence on your left. Cross a stile beside a gate and continue, crossing the next stile by a gate, which is between houses. Now follow the lane. You soon join another lane, where you turn LEFT.

3 After about 20 yards, turn RIGHT, crossing a stile by a gate. Continue along the track, which bends left. Pass agate opn the left, then go RIGHT through a gateway. Walk across the field and cross the stile opposite. Walk over the footbridge and continue ahead, towards the right-hand side of a prominent house. Cross two stiles and walk HALF-LEFT to a gate.

4 Go through this and turn RIGHT along a lane. Follow the lane when it bends left, ignoring the track ahead. Continue ahead to a junction by Affcot Manor Farm. Go ahead through a gate by barns and continue ahead and slightly left over a field to a stile, which you cross. **The farmer here often uses thin electrified fences. Make sure you keep well clear as you duck under them, and WARN YOUR CHILDREN.** Maintain your direction, crossing the next stile, and continue towards buildings. Carry on ahead towards the central point of extensive farm buildings and silos. Walk along the green strip between the buildings, climb steps through the yard, then go through two gates to join a road.

5 Carry straight on. When the road bends to the right by the red-brick house 'Ireland', continue ahead. When the fence and trees on your right end, maintain your direction over the field. Keep to the right of a hedge and through trees to reach a footbridge and a stile. Cross these and continue ahead over another large field. Cross a stile and footbridge and continue, bearing slightly LEFT to reach a gate and an old bridge. Go through the gate, carefully cross the bridge and continue, again bearing slightly LEFT. You reach a stile in the fence to your left. Cross this, cross an old stone bridge and then the stile directly AHEAD. Walk AHEAD over the field, ignoring a stile over to the left. Head for the gap between two large clumps of trees, to reach a stile. Cross it and bear HALF-RIGHT to a stile beside a gate. Cross this and now walk with the fence on your left. Cross the stile in the corner of the field and turn RIGHT to follow a narrow path through trees to reach a stile. Cross this and continue diagonally across a field to reach a stile beside a gate. Cross this and turn HALF-

RIGHT to walk across a small field. Cross a stile to reach the entrance to *Acton Scott Historic Working Farm near Church Stretton. Try to make time to visit this friendly and informal museum where farming life, as it was at the turn of the century, is faithfully re-created amongst a charming collection of buildings. Open Tue-Fri 10.00-16.30. Weekends & B.Hols 10.30-17.00. Closed Mon. Café open to non-visitors. Charge.*

6 Leave Acton Scott and turn LEFT along the road, sharing the route with the 'Wagoners Wander'. Pass a gate on your right, then turn RIGHT opposite the entrance to Acton Scott Farm. Follow the track down to a stile beside a gate. Cross this and turn sharp RIGHT to go through a gate and along an old lane. When you emerge from the lane turn RIGHT to walk with the hedge on your right. Pass through a gate and continue down the path between trees. Descend to a gate, go through and cross a small bridge. Go RIGHT to follow the hedge on the right to the other side of the field to reach a gate. Go through then turn RIGHT to cross a brook and enter trees. Climb the track uphill, go through a gate and continue AHEAD, with a hedge on your right. Leave the field through the gate ahead and follow the track. Join a lane and turn LEFT.

7 Follow the lane as it turns right, and then left. When you reach a 'T' junction, cross the stile which faces you and cross the field, keeping to the edge of the dip to the right, as you head for the stile in the far corner. Cross this stile and cross the lane.

8 Follow the path immediately opposite the stile just crossed, now following the 'Jack Mytton Way'. Go through a gate and continue downhill, beside a stream. Soon you will step across this stream to reach a small waymarked metal gate. Go through this and continue downhill. Carry on ahead across a field, to join a fence on your left. Go through two gates and continue ahead. Go through a gate and walk between houses. You join a road and continue along the track to the right. When you join a road, turn LEFT. At the end of the road turn RIGHT, cross the road and walk to the main road. To reach Church Stretton Station, cross the main road and continue ahead.

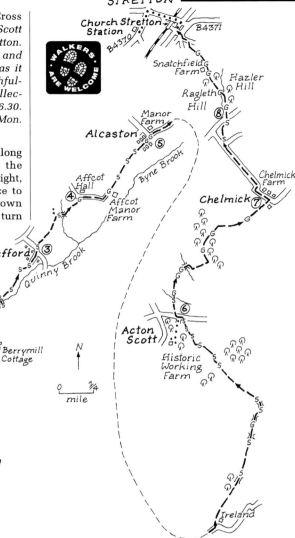

WALK 4

FORTIFICATIONS OLD, & NOT QUITE SO OLD

DESCRIPTION This 5½ mile walk explores two fortifications – the stunningly romantic fortified manor house at Stokesay and the massive embankments of Norton Camp, an iron age hill-fort overlooking the valley. Between the two you will pass through some splendid woodland, and there is the added bonus of a fine church, which is kept open for visitors each day. Allow about 3½ hours for walking, as you will have to tackle a substantial, but steady, climb – and add on some extra time for visits.

START Craven Arms SO432830.

Leave Craven Arms Station from the southbound platform and walk ahead to the main road, where you turn RIGHT. Walk beside this main road, passing three mini-roundabouts and the Craven Arms Hotel. Pass another mini-roundabout at the junction with Clun Road, and continue along Ludlow Road. After passing an apartment block, turn RIGHT into Dodds Lane and keep ahead through housing. Pass under the railway to reach a stile by a gate. Cross the stile and veer LEFT, to walk with a fence and a hedge on your left. Cross the stile in the field corner and turn LEFT, to walk again with the fence and hedge on your left. Cross a stile by a gate and maintain your direction, with the hedge on your left. You reach the railway line on your left. Walk beside it for a short distance then turn LEFT to pass underneath it in a tunnel, to be confronted with a splendid view of Stokesay Castle. Continue ahead, passing a pond to your right, to reach a gate. Go through and turn LEFT. The entrance to both The Church of St John the Baptist and Stokesay Castle is on your right. *During the 13thC wool was one of England's major exports, and the Marches were a major wool-producing area. The tenancy of Stokesay was sold to Lawrence of Ludlow, the leading wool merchant in the area, in 1281 and it*

is thought that he began building Stokesay Castle soon afterwards. It was subjected to a siege during the Civil War, and captured by the Parliamentarians. The Royalists took refuge in the church (see below), which was partially demolished during the skirmish which followed.
In 1647 the Castle was ordered to be 'slighted', or levelled, but fortunately, with the exception of the walls being lowered, little else was done. A detailed guide book is available, and this explains the features of the building in great detail. You can also use an 'audio guide', again available from the shop. Open 10.00-18.00 Apr-Sept, 10.00-16.00 Oct, 10.00-16.00 Weekends only Nov-Mar. Charge. The Church of St John the Baptist was built by the Say family as the chapel for Stokesay Castle. Among the building's most appealing features are 'The Ten Commandments', with Moses and Aaron, painted on the north wall. This charming church is open every day.

2 Now continue along the lane, which bends to the right and joins the main road, where you turn RIGHT. Cross the bridge over the River Onny, then carefully cross the road (it is busy) and just beyond 'Castle View' turn LEFT. After about 25 yards, turn RIGHT to cross a stile and walk with a hedge on your left. Climb steps, cross a stile and turn RIGHT, to follow a clear path through woodland, which curves right to a track. Go LEFT.

3 The track reaches a gate. Go through and walk up the track, taking the first turning to the LEFT. When the track forks, take the RIGHT fork along Rotting Lane (a rough track). At the next fork, go to the RIGHT and continue. You leave the woods through a gateway. Continue, with trees to your right. Gradually a fine view opens up to your right. Cross the stile by a gate on your RIGHT at the end of the woods and turn LEFT, to walk with the hedge on your left.

4 You reach a gate – do not go through, but turn LEFT to cross a stile and walk at the field's edge. Go through a gate and continue, as the track bends to the left.

5 Walk by Whettleton Farm to turn RIGHT, and walk along a lane. The lane bends to the right and reaches a stile by a gate. Cross the stile and turn LEFT, to walk, with the fence and hedge on your left, down to a small footbridge – ignore the gate and path to the left. Cross this and continue ahead to reach a more substantial footbridge, with white gates at each end. Cross this and

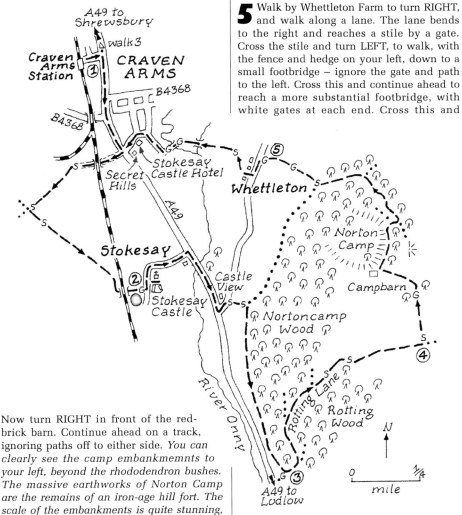

Now turn RIGHT in front of the red-brick barn. Continue ahead on a track, ignoring paths off to either side. *You can clearly see the camp embankmemnts to your left, beyond the rhododendron bushes. The massive earthworks of Norton Camp are the remains of an iron-age hill fort. The scale of the embankments is quite stunning, and the views, where there is a break in the trees, are splendid.* The track descends more steeply. Now be vigilant to look for a green track off to the RIGHT as the track bends left. Descend again, ignoring paths off to the right, until you reach a stile on your RIGHT. Cross it and walk downhill, with a fence to your left. *There is a fine view over Craven Arms here.* Go through sa gateway and keep ahead across a field and down a small hollow, to a gate. Go through the gate and turn LEFT.

continue along a lane, turning RIGHT into Newton. Turn LEFT by the pelican crossing to reach the Stokesay Castle Hotel on your left. Now turn RIGHT at the main road, by the excellent Secret Hills Discovery Centre (well worth a visit – *open Tue-Sun*), to pass the mini-roundabouts and return to the station.

THE QUIETEST PLACES UNDER THE SUN

DESCRIPTION Passing through gentle and attractive countryside, this 6½ mile walk visits two pretty villages in the valley of the River Clun, which are celebrated in A E Housman's famous poem 'A Shropshire Lad':
'Clunton and Clunbury,
Clungunford and Clun,
Are the quietest places
Under the Sun'
Both villages visited, Clungunford and Clunbury, have fine churches. You can, of course, undertake the walk in either direction, although starting from Hopton Heath makes for a gentler climb up the single significant hil. Allow about 4 hours for this walk.
START Hopton Heath SO380774 or Broome SO399809.

1 Leave Hopton Heath Station by climbing the steps and turn RIGHT to walk along the road ahead towards Clungunford. When the road bends left at a junction, continue straight ahead through a kissing gate. Veer to the right when the fence on the right ends, passing trees on your left and descending towards the River Clun to reach a footbridge. Cross this, go through a gap in the fence ahead, then turn HALF-LEFT to walk across a field to a gate. Go through and follow the lane up to the road.

2 Turn LEFT and walk along the road. When you reach a road junction, turn LEFT to walk through Clungunford, a quiet village of timbered houses and converted barns. Pass St Cuthbert's church on the right. *Most of St Cuthbert's Church dates from around 1300, although the tower was added in 1895 by E. Turner of Leicester, who also built the timber porch. The oldest part of the building is probably the north chancel chapel.* Cross the bridge over the River Clun and continue.

Housman mentioned the River Clun:

*'In valleys of springs and rivers,
By Ony and Teme and Clun,
the country for easy livers,
The quietest under the sun'*

Turn RIGHT by the Rocke Tea Rooms (*and you could, of course, stop for refreshment here*). Ignore the first gate on the right, but turn RIGHT at the road junction, to pass Highfield. Continue along the lane, turning LEFT to pass under the Heart of Wales Line. Follow the lane.

3 Pass through a gate and continue with a fence to your left. Cross a stile on the left and then veer to the RIGHT to reach an other stile. Cross this and turn LEFT to walk along a shallow hollow to reach an old gateway (there is no gate). Turn RIGHT to follow the green track uphill to a gate before a barn. Go through and continue upwards, with the hedge now on your right. Turn around to enjoy the view, then continue, going through the next gate. Follow the track upwards with the fence on the left to the next gate. Go through and continue ahead to a gate. Go through and continue to walk down an old hollow lane, enjoying another splendid view, this time looking over the pretty village of Clunbury. Go through a kissing gate. Continue downhill, eventually reaching a metal gate. Go through and continue to the road.

4 Continue AHEAD, ignoring the turning to your right. You reach a staggered crossroads – here you should turn RIGHT to continue the walk, but you can go straight ahead to explore Clunbury and visit St Swithin's Church if you wish. *Standing in close proximity to its secular neighbours, St Swithin's Church is a bold building with a battlemented tower, probably built during the 13thC. The nave roof is a fine timber construction, typical of this area.* Continue along the lane, ignoring a signposted bridge over the river to your left. When the lane turns sharp left to cross a bridge, continue AHEAD along the lane. When the lane ends, continue AHEAD, passing through a waymarked gate,

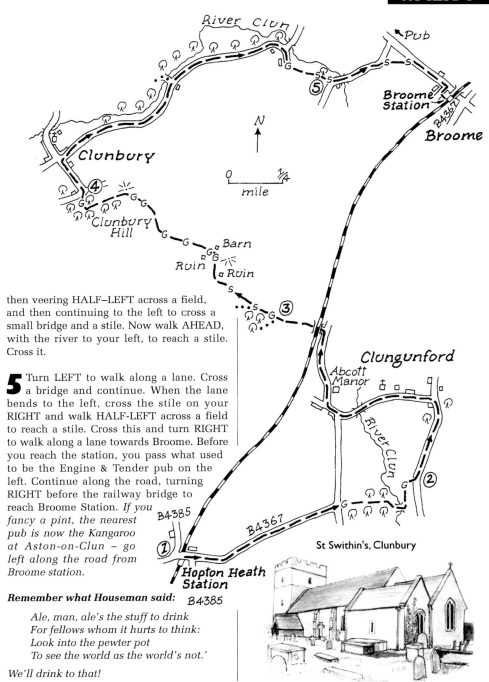

then veering HALF–LEFT across a field, and then continuing to the left to cross a small bridge and a stile. Now walk AHEAD, with the river to your left, to reach a stile. Cross it.

5 Turn LEFT to walk along a lane. Cross a bridge and continue. When the lane bends to the left, cross the stile on your RIGHT and walk HALF-LEFT across a field to reach a stile. Cross this and turn RIGHT to walk along a lane towards Broome. Before you reach the station, you pass what used to be the Engine & Tender pub on the left. Continue along the road, turning RIGHT before the railway bridge to reach Broome Station. *If you fancy a pint, the nearest pub is now the Kangaroo at Aston-on-Clun – go left along the road from Broome station.*

Remember what Houseman said:

> Ale, man, ale's the stuff to drink
> For fellows whom it hurts to think:
> Look into the pewter pot
> To see the world as the world's not.'

We'll drink to that!

St Swithin's, Clunbury

A BYWORD FOR TREACHERY

DESCRIPTION This walk follows a lane of some antiquity from Hopton Heath Station to Hopton Castle where the castle ruins have been restored by the Hopton Castle Preservation Trust. From here the walk climbs the wooded flanks of Hopton Titterhill through quiet countryside to the Redlake Valley along gentle paths leading into the village of Bucknell. 5½ miles, allow 3½ hours.

START Hopton Heath Station SO776380 or Bucknell Station SO736356.

1 From the platform of Hopton Heath Railway Station climb up steps to a road. Turn LEFT and LEFT again to follow a lane with wide verges towards the village of Hopton Castle. As the road descends look for steps on the RIGHT up to a stile. Cross it and head half LEFT across the field to another stile. Cross this and continue towards a tree. Go through the gate on the left to re-join the road then go RIGHT to a junction in the village and turn LEFT here to the castle.

2 Return to the junction in Hopton Castle but now turn LEFT and walk through the village ignoring turns to the right. Pass the entrance to Upper House Farm on the right and at the next bend go LEFT through a gate into a field. Follow the track through a pasture, and another gate. Continue as it veers LEFT into a wood through a gate. The track bends LEFT up to a junction. Go RIGHT here on the forest track (shared by cyclists).

3 The track leads through the wood and as it descends towards a bend, go LEFT at the fork to rise steadily to join another track. Keep ahead, across a forestry track. Go ahead again with woodland to the left and fields to the right and continue on a green track between a hedge and fence. Continue until Meeroak farm where you go through a gate and turn LEFT. Walk through a gate to the left of barns and ahead on a track.

4 Go through another gate into a wood and turn RIGHT immediately, on to a green path with a hedge to the right. Cross a stile and head half RIGHT across a field to a waymark post at the wood's edge. *There's a wonderful view up the Redlake Valley to Caradoc.* Go RIGHT to drop down to cross a stile by a gate. Descend to cross another stile by a gate. Pass by a dwelling on the left and through wet ground to a stile by a gate. Follow the path with a hedge on the left down to a kissing gate; keep to the left of the buildings on a drive. At this point, go through the barred gate into a field and turn RIGHT. Follow the hedge on the RIGHT to exit through a barred gate.

5 Turn LEFT on the road and as it bends RIGHT, before a bridge, go LEFT through a gate by a signpost. Proceed ahead to follow the river bank to cross a stile. Continue to a corner then go half LEFT across a water meadow to rise to a stile. Cross it to join a wider path. Turn RIGHT through a wood and leave through a gate. Continue ahead to go through a gate to Bridgend Lane. This joins the main road through the village.

6 Go LEFT to pass by the Baron Country Inn and the road bends RIGHT, over a bridge, to reach Bucknell church. Beforehand, go LEFT along the path by the river to another road with a garage on the left. Turn RIGHT here to pass the Sitwell Arms on the way to the level crossing and Bucknell Railway Station. There's also a bus, 738/740, which runs direct to Ludlow or Knighton from here and a summer only 783 bus which runs at weekends (see slowtravel-marches.blogspot.co.uk for updates).

Hopton Castle was in a poor state of repair until recently when a group of dedicated local people raised funds and bid for a grant to restore its future for generations to come. The formidable 14thC keep is now intact but this castle is know for an atrocity carried out in the English Civil War when a revengeful Royalist army slaughtered many of the Parliamentarians who had initially flaunted the normal rules of engagement at a siege played out here. Hence, in

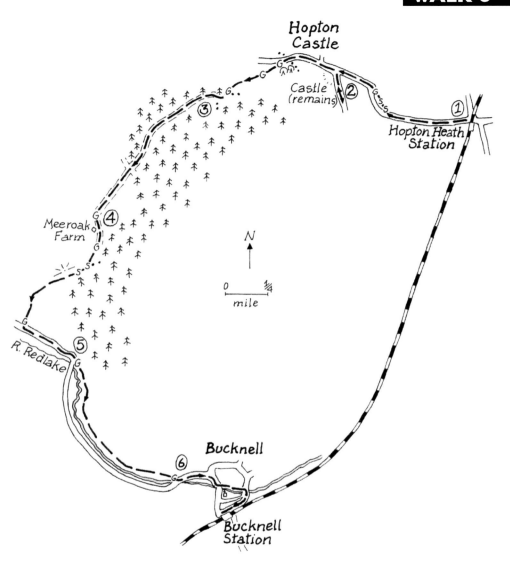

Hopton
Castle

Castle
(remains)

Hopton Heath
Station

Meeroak
Farm

N

0 ——— ¼
mile

R. Redlake

Bucknell

Bucknell
Station

the 17thC, Hopton Castle became a byword for treachery.

Bucknell station was built in 1860 to serve a growing agricultural settlement at the time. The village is a great place to start or end a walk as it has two shops and the Sitwell Arms and Baron Country Inn. The Sitwell Arms is located within 3 minutes walk of the station and is open all day; it welcomes walkers.

WALK 7

WALKING WITH OFFA

DESCRIPTION This station to station walk from Bucknell to Knighton follows tracks and lanes through to the hillside hamlet of Stowe with its lovely church, then over fields to Kinsley Woods and the gap town of Knighton, where a visit to the Offa's Dyke Centre is a must. 5 miles, allow 3 hours.
START Bucknell Station SO035736 or Knighton Station SO292724.

1 From Bucknell station go LEFT over the crossing and then RIGHT to pass the Sitwell Arms. Turn next LEFT along a path which borders the River Redlake. Follow this to Bucknell Church (on the left) and a road where the post office is opposite. Go LEFT and then RIGHT to cross the road. Rise up steps and through a kissing gate to the right of a house. Go ahead at first then veer RIGHT to a kissing gate. Go ahead through two more fields and kissing gates before going RIGHT to a gate onto the road.

2 Turn LEFT and at the corner keep ahead along Daffodil Lane with the recreational ground on the right. This rises to a junction. Keep LEFT to leave the tarmac and at the junction at the top proceed ahead with a fence to the left. As the track bends right keep ahead and ignore paths either side. The track dips down to a road at Cubbatt.

3 Turn RIGHT and follow this lane to a junction at Weston where you can just see the old overshot waterwheel at the farm on the right. However, keep ahead at the junction and follow the lane as it dips down to the railway beneath a plantation on the right and a small nature reserve on the left. The lane then begins to rise up to a corner where you proceed over a stile ahead into a field. Continue with the hedge on the right to reach two gates. Go through the one on the LEFT and continue ahead to a gate before farm buildings. Go through it and then RIGHT to go through another. Turn LEFT and

follow the hedge to a stile on the LEFT with steps down to a track. Turn RIGHT to pass farm buildings onto a road in the hamlet of Stowe. Turn RIGHT if you wish to visit the church.

4 Otherwise, go LEFT and immediately RIGHT to pass through a gate (the one on the left) along a green track but within 50 yards go RIGHT through a barred gate into a field. Continue to another barred gate and once through go half LEFT up the field to no less than three gates. Turn LEFT to go through the one on the very LEFT and head down the field with the hedge on the left. Go through two barred gates and at the third to continue ahead again but with the hedge now on the right. Pass through a fourth gate but then take care as you cross this main road.

5 Cross a stile and footbridge. Aim for a point about 30 yards to the right of a far left top corner of the field. Cross a stile, climb steps and then go LEFT on the forestry track in Kinsley Wood. However, cut next RIGHT along a path which runs through the wood parallel to the road below. This descends to main road. Cross this to access Knighton Railway Station.

6 However, if you have time it is worth extending the route to the Offa's Dyke Visitor Centre. *These are the directions:* Go

14

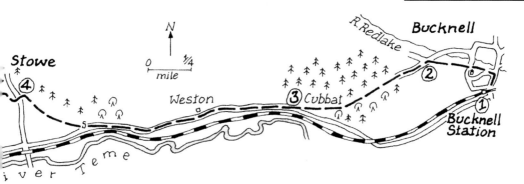

LEFT over the railway bridge and proceed along Station Road towards the town centre but make a RIGHT turn up Church Road to pass the church of St Edward and then ahead along Church Street into West Street where you go RIGHT for the Centre. It is a ten minute walk.

*T*he Offa's Dyke Visitor Centre is home to the Offa's Dyke Association, which has worked tirelessly over the years to explain the history of the dyke and to conserve it for future generations. It has also done much to promote walking along Offa's Dyke Path and other paths in the borderlands. The dyke was built in the 8th century by the powerful overload of Mercia, King Offa and is a marvel to see. There's an exhibition and tourist information at the Centre – open daily 10.00-17.00 hours (16.00 in winter, closed winter Sundays). In recent times walking routes have been promoted under the banner of Walking with Offa with several based in the Bucknell area; try number 12 which leads to the rare Parlour pub, the Sun Inn at Leintwardine!

Offa's Dyke Centre, Knighton

KING ARTHUR & A FOXY TALE

DESCRIPTION This moderate 6 mile walk between Llangunllo and Knucklas stations affords fine views of Knucklas viaduct which carries the Heart of Wales line in thirteen strides across a peaceful Heyop valley. It also visits the site of a castle associated with King Arthur, and which was later used by the Normans. The walk follows Glyndŵr's Way to Bailey Hill then offers glorious views on the descent to Knucklas village where a short detour takes you to the castle. There's also an opportunity to call into the village pub, appropriately called The Castle Inn, which is renowned for hosting 'Folk Down the Track', an evening of folk for train travellers. 6 miles, allow 3 hours.
START Llangunllo SO210730 or Knucklas SO254741.

| *Llangunllo Station stands close to the summit of the line, which reaches a height of 980 feet just a little north of here by Llyncoch Tunnel, itself 1935 feet long. It is said that if you look down the track from Llangunllo you will notice a slight kink in the line, caused by a farmer who 'adjusted' the surveyors' pegs in order to preserve his access to a spring!* From Llangunllo station go LEFT down the road and under the railway bridge. As the road bends right keep ahead through a gate into a field. Continue with a fence to the right and proceed down a green lane curving LEFT to a stream. Cross the footbridge and rise to go through a gate. Go ahead on a lane to reach a road. Cross it and go ahead again down a lane into the village of Llangunllo where you will find the welcoming Greyhound pub on the right.

2 Turn LEFT at the junction and as the road bends right by Lugg View go LEFT and then RIGHT up a fenced path. Cross a stile by a gate to enter a pasture. Keep LEFT and rise to a gate. Go through it and continue to climb to a next gate. Cross a track and go half RIGHT as the path leads into scrub and

to a gate. Go through it. Turn LEFT on the road for about 100 metres then go RIGHT through a gate. Head half LEFT across a field to go through a gate and then half RIGHT to go through a gateway and then a gate beyond. Keep ahead across a field to a gate which you pass through. Continue ahead on the track and descend towards Cefnsuran farm.

3 Go through another gate and then turn LEFT and in about 15 yards turn RIGHT through a gate to reach a tarmac drive. Go LEFT through gate by a cattle grid. Go ahead at crossroads of tracks until you reach a junction. Turn RIGHT. There are three gates; select the middle one and follow the track to a bridge and gate. Once through continue ahead up the field to a gate. Head half

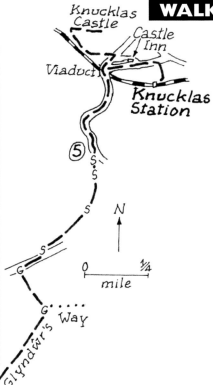

RIGHT to a waymark post and track. Go LEFT on the track to ford a stream. Then proceed half RIGHT to climb up to a gate. Turn RIGHT along the green track, through another gate and ahead again. Ignore the gate by the old railway wagon and continue with the hedge to your right to climb up the field to the top corner where there's a crossing of tracks.

4 Proceed ahead in the next field to go through a gate and then by sheep pens. The track descends to a gate. Go through it and note a waymark indicating that Glyndŵr's Way is peeling off towards Knighton. However, you keep ahead to a gate. Go through it on to a lonely lane. Turn RIGHT to walk along the lane but look for a signpost and stile on the LEFT. The views over the Heyop Valley and Knucklas are exceptional from here. Cross the stile and go half LEFT across the hillside pasture. Cross the next stile and continue in a similar direction to a stile next to a bridle gate. Keep ahead along a line of hawthorns on your right. Cross a stile and dip down between gorse bushes to cross a stile onto a lane.

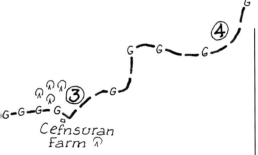

5 Turn LEFT to walk down the lane which descends, steeply in places, to Knucklas to pass under the viaduct. For those seeking to see the castle keep LEFT at the fork and take the next turn LEFT up by the telephone kiosk. At the top of the lane, as it bends RIGHT, go RIGHT as waymarked up to the castle managed by the Knucklas Castle Community Land Project. Otherwise go RIGHT at the fork to pass by the Castle inn and then next RIGHT for the station.

*C*nwclas Castle, *standing on Castle Hill, above Knucklas, occupies a strategic position overlooking a point where the Ffrwdwen Book joins the River Teme. The hill was originally topped with an iron-age hillfort, and was associated in legend with King Arthur and Queen Guinevere. Crowned later with a stone keep, this last fortification was begun by Ralph Mortimer and completed in 1242 by his son Roger. It was taken by Owain Glyndŵr's army in 1402, during that last great flourish of Welsh independence. Now very little of the castle remains.*

*T*he Castle Inn *is a friendly and welcoming pub, where you will, as often as not, be greeted by the genial host amidst warm wood panelling, stone walls and slate floors. A large stove stands ready should the weather turn chilly. Real ales are served, and the bar meals are both excellently prepared and reasonably priced.*

WALK 9

ON THE TRAIL OF GLYNDŴR

DESCRIPTION Climbing steadily from Llangunllo Station to a height of 1640 feet this route explores the remote uplands where Glyndŵr's Way passes close to the source of the River Lugg. You will cross Beacon Hill Common, a fine expanse of land where there is the opportunity to see some of the rarer upland birds, and enjoy splendid views. The walk is 5 miles long 'station to station' if you catch a train at Llanbister Road, but you can extend the route to 8 miles by returning to your starting point along quiet lanes. Allow about 3 hours for the 'station to station' route, or 4–5 hours for the circular route. There is a pub, The Greyhound, at Llangunllo.

START Llangunllo SO210730 or Llanbister Road SO174716.

1 Leave Llangunllo Station and turn RIGHT to walk along the lane. When you reach a triangular junction continue AHEAD along a 'No Through Road', starting to climb gently and eventually passing 'Ferley' on your right. Go through a gate and continue along the lane. Pass Ferley Hall on your left and continue. Go through a gate and continue, then go through another two gates to pass to the right of Upper Ferley, then take the lane ahead (don't go to the right!).

2 Go through a gate and turn RIGHT along a track, which continues your steady climb. Turn around to enjoy a fine view opening up behind you. Stay on the track – you pass a signpost to your right, then climb to a gate and continue. IGNORE the gate on your left into woodland.

3 Turn LEFT immediately after it, to walk over Beacon Hill Common. *This common is owned by the Crown Estate, and comprises 1889 hectares (4667 acres) of upland moor, parts of which are designated as Sites of Special Scientific Interest. There are ancient monuments: tumuli and the Short Ditch, which is passed on this walk.* Walk along the clear track, which cuts through the Short Ditch. Gradually excellent views open up to your right. You are now walking on an exposed section of Glyndŵr's Way, a National Trail which celebrates this Welsh revolutionary. When the track forks, take the LEFT fork as waymarked and continue along the green track for about 400 yards until you reach an indistinct cross-tracks.

4 You can check your position by looking over to your right, where you will see the roof of a barn about a quarter-of-a-mile away. Turn LEFT here and follow the track over a small hill. Continue ahead as the track becomes just a path, and pass to the right of a small lake. When this lake is immediately on your left, start to veer slightly left and look out for a clear track, which starts to descend into a small cwm. You will cross a marshy patch, which is in fact the source of the River Lugg (although it can dry up during the summer). Now veer LEFT to walk to the right of the river and parallel to it, staying above the gorge and following a distinct track. Gradually the river starts to head away to your left, but you stay on what is now a clear track, starting to descend *and enjoying the sweeping views ahead.* Eventually you reach a gate, which you go through to continue along a hedged track, keeping a radio mast ahead.

5 Go through the gate at the bottom and turn RIGHT. When you reach a road continue AHEAD (don't turn left), then turn LEFT at the road junction, to walk along a lane. When the lane veers to the right and just before it starts to descend, go through the angled gate on the LEFT and walk DIAGONALLY across the field. As you start to descend, walk towards the gap in the trees ahead. Ignore a gate on your left, and walk down to a gate in the hollow ahead. Go through and walk down to a gate on the RIGHT. Go through this and walk HALF-LEFT to a small footbridge. Cross this and walk slightly RIGHT to reach a stile. Cross this and you are on Llanbister Road Station. You can now catch the train, or walk back to the start along quiet lanes. (Leave the station and turn left. Continue ahead at the first road

Margaret Hanmer and with a 'nest of children'. In 1400 there was discontent in Wales and Scotland and, on 16 September, Owain was proclaimed Prince of Wales, encouraged by Welsh hatred for the English King and his Marcher Lords. By the 24th they had raided several towns and were closing upon Welshpool when they were routed near Shrewsbury. Henry VI's army arrived the next day, and subsequently subdued the rebellion. All the rebels, except Owain, were pardoned. Rebellion re-occurred in 1401, with Conwy Castle being burned. Owain raised an army, and Henry responded, strengthening garrisons and reinforcing castles. A comet which appeared

junction, turn left at the next, and left again at Pye Corner, to return to Llangunllo.)

Who was Owain Glyndŵr? In 1284 Edward I completed England's conquest of Wales, when Llywelyn was killed in a skirmish with English forces at Cilmeri, near Builth Wells. Owain ap Gruffydd, Owain Glyndŵr, was born around 1359, the son of Gryffydd Fychan and a descendant of the royal house of Powys. He became Squire to Henry Bolingbroke, King Richard's cousin, and during this period he would have learned his fighting skills. His military career over, he settled near Sycharth in a moated wooden house, married to

in the sky in 1402 was taken as an omen, since its tail was said to point towards Wales. Owain's rebellion grew, defeating the English at Pilleth, near Knighton, at a place called Bryn Glas. Owain then moved south, and also blockaded the castles at Harlech and Caernarfon. By 1404 Owain had secured Wales, taken Harlech Castle and established a Parliament in Machynlleth. Eventually King Henry became ill, and gave Prince Henry a free hand to campaign, successfully, in Wales, turning Owain into a fugitive. In 1407 the rebellion faded through starvation and a lack of funds. By 1410 it was all over. Owain Glyndŵr faded from history, and perhaps died on the 20th September 1415 at Monnington-on-Wye, or on an exposed mountain ridge in Gwynedd. Or maybe he ended his days quietly at Pwllirch, Darowen.

WALK 10

UN-COMMONLY GOOD WALKING

DESCRIPTION Walking from one wonderfully remote station, Llanbister Road, to another, Dolau, this 6½ mile route crosses Coxhead Bank Common and passes by the mound of Castell Cymaran (private). It is easy walking, allowing you plenty of time to enjoy a serenely peaceful part of Radnorshire. If you are feeling energetic, you can return to your staring point along narrow and quiet country lanes, lined with summer flowers, and autumn blackberries. Allow about 3½ hours for a one way walk, or about 6 hours if you walk back along the lanes to Llanbister Road. There are no pubs on this walk, so bring refreshments – you are sure to find a pleasant spot for a picnic if the weather is fine.

START Llanbister Road SO174716 or Dolau SO140671.

1 Climb the steps from Llanbister Road Station, go through the gate and turn LEFT. At the road junction turn RIGHT (as signed for Dolau). Continue along the lane to reach houses at Cwm-y-gaist, and turn RIGHT then pass by 'Cwm Islwyn' on a track after Cwm Villa. Continue straight ahead to cross over the railway line on a wide bridge. Go through a gate and turn HALF-LEFT to walk along a shallow dip in the field. Ford a stream (there are some stepping stones to carefully step across if the water is high) and go through the RIGHT-HAND gate, to walk with a fence on your left. Go through a gate and continue ahead, walking beside a very fine, but overgrown, hollow green lane. Go through the gate ahead and maintain your direction over the field up to the top corner, to go through a gate where you join a farm track and turn RIGHT.

2 Cross a cattle-grid and turn HALF-LEFT to walk across Coxhead Bank Common. *This is a splendid expanse of land, offering fine views to the south-west. You should, of course, keep to the right-of-way across here, since the popular belief that common land is owned by the public is incorrect. Most medieval villages had several acres on the edge of the settlement set aside for the use of the villagers, but all this common land was actually privately owned, either by the Lord of the Manor, collectively by the local villagers or perhaps even by a city corporation. What is held 'in common' by certain local individuals or their families is the right to use this land. If you were such a tenant, you were known as 'a commoner', and, as such, had rights: of pasture – to graze specified livestock; of estovers – to gather and take wood (but not fell trees); in the soil – to take sand, coal or minerals; of turbary – to dig peat for fuel; and of piscary – to catch fish from ponds or streams. This extended only to that which the ground produced naturally, ie. there was no right to plant crops, and there were often seasonal limitations. Usually 'Bye Law men' were appointed annually from the tenants of the common, and it was their job to care for hedges, gates, drains and ditches.* Continue, descending gradually and keeping an infant stream to your right, then veering right to walk down to the road. During the summer the path is hidden amdst bracken up to 6 feet tall. (As an alternative you continue along the farm track until it meets a road, where you turn left.) Turn LEFT and continue ahead, ignoring a road off to the left. Pass the substantial motte and bailey of Castell Cymaran on your left. *The substantial mound and embankment of Castell Cymaran can still be seen here, and it is thought that building began around 1093, instigated by Ralph Mortimer. By 1134 it had been destroyed by Madog ab Idnerth. It was rebuilt in 1144 by Hugh Mortimer, and taken six years later by Cadwallon ap Madog. When Cadwallon died the castle was subjected to many disputes, and was taken and retaken by opposing forces. Bishop Giles Braose of Hereford and Llywelyn ap Iorwerth destroyed it in 1215, but in 1240 it was again rebuilt, and occupation certainly continued until 1360. None of the castle buildings remain. The ground is private: please do not go through the gate.* Continue along this quiet lane, passing Lower Sign farm, with its fine wooden barns, also on the left.

3 At the road junction turn LEFT. When the tarmac lane bends to the left, continue AHEAD through a signed wooden gate. Walk along the hollow lane, with the hedge on your left. Go through a gate, walking now with a fence to the right, then turn RIGHT at the far side of a field, to walk along a wide track. Go through a gate and continue ahead along a track. Pass through another gate, and then another, keeping the modern breeze-block and timber barns to the right, to follow the track to the right and left to descend through Far Hall farmyard. The track bends to the left, you leave the farmyard through a gateway and then immediately turn RIGHT down a green lane.

4 Cross a bridge and go through the gate into a large field to walk slightly LEFT across a field towards two gates side-by-side in the far corner. Go through the newer of the two gates and continue ahead along a track. You reach a gate ahead, with a gate to the right. Go through the gate AHEAD, leaving the track, to walk with the hedge to the right. Go through a gate and walk ahead to the far corner of the field by the railway.

5 Cross the stile and then immediately turn LEFT to cross a fence stile. Turn RIGHT to cross the railway bridge, climb the stile and turn LEFT to walk with the fence to your left. Go through a gate and continue ahead, passing through another gate, with the railway line to your left. Walk ahead

to cross a stile and pass to the left of the chapel and cross another stile. Turn LEFT to arrive at Dolau Station.

It is hard to believe that the splendidly well-cared for Dolau Station is just a 'request only' stop, since it has fine floral decorations, a plate-layers trolley, a Victorian clock and lamp, and a splendid little waiting room containing a fascinating display of 'best-kept station' awards, historic photographs of the railway and framed poems. The station was opened in 1864, and once had a small goods and coal yard, and a signal box. By 1983 it had become very run down, prompting the formation of the Dolau Station Action Group, who are to be applauded for all the excellent work they have done.

You can now take the train from Dolau Station, or enjoy a pleasant walk along very quiet lanes back to Llanbister Road Station, by continuing along the road, with the station to your right. Take the first turning on the LEFT, ignore the next left, and then turn LEFT again at the following road junction. Just continue along this lane to eventually return to your starting point.

WALK II
TAKING THE WATERS

DESCRIPTION The charming, spacious, elegant and genteel spa town of Llandrindod Wells grew from a few scattered cottages. Promoted by Dr Wessel Linden's treatise on the health-giving effects of 'taking the waters' in 1756, the enterprise lasted some 40 years before falling into disuse. It was the building of the railway in 1865, which fortunately coincided with a Victorian obsession with drinking mineral waters, that finally brought about the town's rapid growth. This moderate 7 mile walk explores the town, visits the lake, St Michael's church and Cefnllys Castle, and returns via the excellent Cycle Museum. Allow about 4 hours.
START Llandrindod Wells SO059613.

I When you arrive at Llandrindod Station, make sure you visit the *Signal Box Museum, which is open 11.00-12.30 & 13.30-15.00 Whitsun, Fri & Sat, Sun when there is a train service, and all week during Victorian Week, which is staged in August each year.* Now cross over the footbridge and turn LEFT. Fork RIGHT into the High Street, and go straight ahead at the roundabout to enter Rock Park & Spa. Walk ahead then fork RIGHT over the footbridge to visit the Pump Room. *One hundred years ago, during the season, you would have had to join a queue in order to take the waters, which were dispensed in The Pump Room, and were thought to have such a beneficial effect on your health. Next door there is a fine café.* Now leave The Pump Room and walk ahead, with the stream on your left, *to visit the Chalybeate Spring, opened in 1819.* Walk back up the slope and take the tarmac path uphill to your LEFT. When you reach a path cross-roads, by a street lamp, turn LEFT. Cross the footbridge and

turn RIGHT to walk through a subway under the railway, fork left and follow the path over a small bridge to reach Temple Street. Carefully cross the road, walk up the road almost opposite and continue ahead into the park, passing the skateboard ramp on your left. When you reach a road, turn RIGHT. Pass the remains of Capel Maelog on your left.

2 When you reach The Lake, turn RIGHT, to walk with the water on your left, passing the café and craft shop. *The lake was created out of a bog in 1872-3, and is overlooked by Llandrindod Wells old parish church, dating from 1291.* Turn LEFT when you reach the road and continue by the lake. Stay by the lake at the next road junction and follow the road as it bends left, until you reach the Picnic Area sign.

3 At the corner, as the road bends left, follow the track on the right but, as it bends left, keep right on a woodland path. Where paths cross go LEFT, with a fence on your left. AT the next junction, before a stile, turn

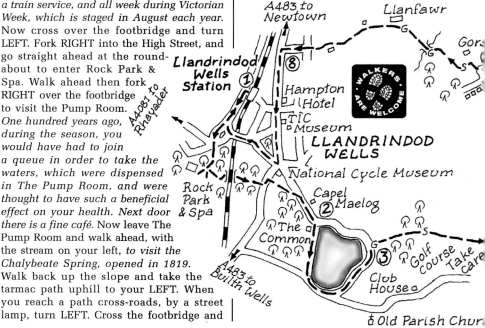

22

RIGHT and climb up through the wood. The path veers left and then right before a large oak tree. Continue to climb ahead through bracken to a stile. Cross it and keep ahead across a field to a a kissing gate. Go through it and continue ahead to a stile by a gate. Go through this and continue ahead to another stile, which you cross. Walk uphill to a cairn, and enjoy the views, then continue down to a stile in the field corner.

4 Cross this stile and turn LEFT to walk along a lane. Follow this lane until it becomes a track, passing organic vegetable gardens on the right. When this track veers right and ascends, cross the stile on the LEFT and follow the track, with a fence to your right. Go through a gate and walk along a clear track through woods. When the path forks, take either route to reach a kissing gate. Go through and continue to reach a road. Turn LEFT then, after about 10 yards, turn RIGHT.

5 Go through the gate head and cross the Shaky Bridge. *There is a fine painting of it in the town museum. Now follow the clear path to visit the church, which stands in a wonderful setting, completely isolated in a valley. St Michael's Church is enclosed by a circular churchyard, indicating pre-Christian origins. Now leave the churchyard and return to the Shaky Bridge, enjoying the view of Castle Hill over to your left, which is topped with the fallen remains of two castles.* Cross the bridge, go through the gate and immediately turn RIGHT to go through a kissing gate, then immediately LEFT to climb a stile. Walk diagonally uphill across a field, veering right around a hollow to reach a stile in the top corner of the field.

6 Cross this stile and turn RIGHT along a lane. Follow the lane as it turns to the left and continue.

7 When the lane bends sharply by a large marker stone, go ahead, ignoring a track off to the left. Turn LEFT as directed by a finger post, before reaching a house. You come to a stile, which you cross and turn RIGHT, to walk along a narrow path by a fence. Veer left with the fence, and then turn RIGHT to go through a kissing gate and cross a small stream. Now continue ahead, with a hedge on your right. Go through a kissing gate and turn LEFT along a lane. Continue through a gate and walk ahead down Quarry Lane into the town.

8 Turn LEFT at the main road, and pass the Tourist Information Centre and Museum on your left, *containing a fascinating collection of relics of local interest, including a painting of the Old Shaky Bridge and a fine Speed map of the county.* Continue, to reach the National Cycle Museum, *a splendidly presented exhibition of old and new bicycles. Open 10.00-16.00 daily (not Mon Nov-Mar). Charge.* Now leave the Cycle Museum, walk up Spa Road opposite, cross the railway bridge and turn RIGHT to return to the station.

23

WALK 12

THE LLYWELYN MEMORIAL

DESCRIPTION Starting from the tiny village of Cilmery, where you will find a substantial memorial to Prince Llywelyn, this 8½ mile walk visits St Cannen's Church, a charming and well hidden little gem, before finding its way down to the River Wye, which tumbles over stones between wooded banks. Much of the return route follows a quiet country lane, giving splendid views over the Wye Valley. Just before you reach the station you can visit the Prince Llewelyn Inn, a splendidly unspoilt and old-fashioned pub. Allow about 5 hours for this walk.
START Cilmery SO003512.

1 Walk up the lane from Cilmeri Station to the main road and turn RIGHT. Cross the road and, when you reach 'The Old Post Office' (the first dwelling on the left), turn LEFT onto a track after the house, don't follow the track, but go through a kissing gate to the right and walk diagonally across the field as directed by the waymark. When you reach the far corner, turn RIGHT to follow the path, with a stream to your left. Pass through a gap in the trees and continue with the hedge to your left. Cross a stile ahead to enter the churchyard and visit the church. *On the banks of the river Chwefri, the diminutive St Cannen's Church was founded shortly after 500 AD by Cannen, grandson of Brychan Brycheiniog, who was a Christian preacher and King of Morganwy, Gwent and Garthmadryn between about 400-450 AD. It is quite likely that Llywelyn, the last native Prince of Wales, was interred here for a while after being killed at Cefn-y-Bedd, later to become Cilmery (see below). One of the chapel walls, and the font, date from the 12thC: the nave was added in the 17thC. Although restored in 1882 by Lewis Powell of Hereford, it has retained its classic simplicity, and remains a rural gem.*

2 Leave the churchyard through the gate and walk along the lane. Turn LEFT at the junction and continue. Cross the cattle grid, passing a bridge on your left (which can be used in tiomes of flood), to reach a ford. *This ford may well have been in use since Roman times, when it was on the route of a road associated with Sarn Helen.* Cross the stream and continue through a gate into the yard of Neuadd-rhos-Fer farm. Exit through the gate opposite and follow the track until you reach two gates. Go through the RIGHT-HAND gate and follow the track. When you are facing a bridge under the railway, turn LEFT to walk with the railway to your right. THe track rises to a corner where you keep ahead on a green lane

3 Go through a gate before Rhosferig-fawr and immediately turn RIGHT through a gap. Cross the stile and walk with the fence on your left. Ignore the stile ahead and turn RIGHT to walk down the field, beside an obstructed sunken lane. Cross the stile ahead and continue. Go through a gate on your LEFT before Rhosferig-fach. Continue along with the hedge on the right until you reach a stile. Cross another stile onthe opposite side opf the lane. Walk HALF-LEFT across the field. You reach a stile by the railway. Cross this, descend steps and **CAREFULLY cross the railway track, ensuring that there are no trains approaching**. Follow the path through trees and cross the stile. Now walk HALF-LEFT across the field to a break in the fence. Negotiate this break, cross the track and climb the break in the fence opposite. Continue, maintaining your direction. Pass through a short stand of conifers and cross the stile. Turn RIGHT and continue, passing an isolated oak tree to reach a stile ahead.

4 Climb this stile and continue ahead, to cross a well-hidden stile to your RIGHT of buildings. Negotiate another stile and continue. Cross a further stile and carry on. When you reach a stile on your RIGHT, cross it and maintain your direction on a path through woods. The path winds beneath trees to eventually reach a track. Go LEFT through a gate. Follow the clear track over the golf course. When you reach the road, turn LEFT.

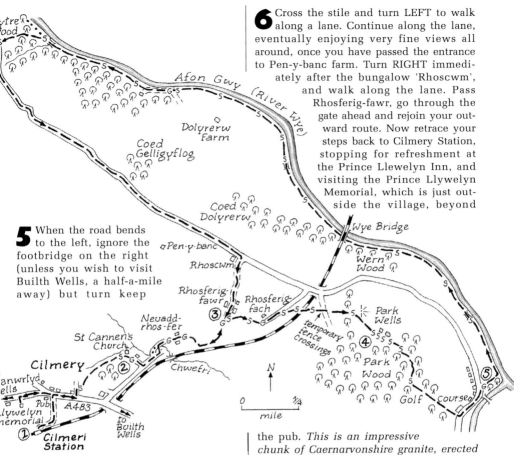

6 Cross the stile and turn LEFT to walk along a lane. Continue along the lane, eventually enjoying very fine views all around, once you have passed the entrance to Pen-y-banc farm. Turn RIGHT immediately after the bungalow 'Rhoscwm', and walk along the lane. Pass Rhosferig-fawr, go through the gate ahead and rejoin your outward route. Now retrace your steps back to Cilmery Station, stopping for refreshment at the Prince Llewelyn Inn, and visiting the Prince Llywelyn Memorial, which is just outside the village, beyond

5 When the road bends to the left, ignore the footbridge on the right (unless you wish to visit Builth Wells, a half-a-mile away) but turn keep ahead through a bridlegate and walk with a fence on your right. The path reaches the riverside and turns LEFT. You then follow the path with the river to your right. You go through several gates before passing under a railway bridge. Cross the stile, go RIGHT through the gate (which is beside a cattle grid) and follow the track. Stay beside the river when the track bends away to the left, up to an exotic wooden riverside retreat. Pass through the garden and cross a stile. Continue, crossing another stile under trees. When you reach a footbridge followed by a stile, cross both then turn LEFT on a distinct track uphill. At the top of the slope maintain your direction across a field to reach a stile.

the pub. *This is an impressive chunk of Caernarvonshire granite, erected in 1956 to mark the spot where Llewelyn, the last native Prince of Wales, was killed. In 1246 he succeeded David, and rebelled against the English in 1282. Beaten, he became a fugitive and initially avoided capture by hiding in Aberedw rocks. He also managed to hoodwink his pursuers by having his horse shod with the horseshoes back-to-front! Llywelyn was eventually taken and killed on the 11th of December 1282 at Cefn-y-Bedd (later Cilmery) by Adam de Francton. His head was sent to London, but his body may have been interred for a while at St Cannen's Church, before being taken to Abbey Cwm-hir. The thirteen oaks which surround the monolith commemorate the thirteen old counties of Wales.*

25

WALK 13

LLANGAMMARCH WELLS & GARTH

DESCRIPTION This 6 mile walk makes a worthwhile circuit encompassing the stations both at Garth and Llangammarch Wells. You will enjoy splendid views of the Eppynt, a vast upland area which has been used by the army since World War II for training, the equally bare but infinitely more peaceful hills to the north, the pleasant valley of the Irfon, remote woodlands and the small spa town of Llangammarch Wells. This circuit should take about 3 hours to complete, although you can just walk station to station either to the north or south of the river. There is a fine pub in Llangammarch Wells, where you can spend some time if you are waiting for a train.

START Either Garth SN954495 or Llangammarch Wells SN936473

1 Leave the station at Garth and walk along the road, passing a 20mph section and the school to reach the main road. Turn LEFT. Walk though the village until you reach a fork in the road. Take the LEFT fork but almost immediately look over to your right for a small brown telephone exchange building. Follow the signed bridleway which leaves a track to the left of this. When you reach a waymarked gate, go through and continue ahead. Pass through a second waymarked gateway and continue ahead, gently climbing. The track now affords fine views to your right. Pass through a small metal gate as the track swings gently to the right. You now descend to a gate, which you go through and carry on, now along the edge of a field with a fence to your right.

2 Go through a gate by an old railway wagon shed, the ruins of Treflys, and a radio mast, and continue ahead along a wide fenced track. Go through a metal gate and continue ahead, enjoying excellent views both to the north and south. You pass through another metal gate to enter a tree-lined section of this wide bridleway. Go through a metal gate and continue ahead. The track begins to gently descend as you pass through another gate, and then another.

At the next gate, which you pass through, you catch a glimpse of the farm buildings of Llwynbrain to the right as your gentle descent continues between trees. As you go through another gate this descent begins to steepen, with the track now being made muddy by the appearance of a stream. Soon you are negotiating very deep ruts, so take care. Pass through a gate where a stream joins the track from the right and carry on ahead to finally pass through a gate to join a tarmac farm road and, maintaining your direction, you cross a bridge over the Afon Cammarch to reach a minor road.

3 Turn LEFT and walk along the road, ignoring a road which leaves to the right. As you climb this hill a strategically placed seat prompts you to turn around for a moment to enjoy the view to the north-west. Continue along the road to descend towards the village, crossing the Afon Cammarch on a bridge overlooked by St Cadmarch's Church, up on a rise to your left.

4 You pass the Cammarch Hotel to your right and walk under the railway, with the station to your left. The road crosses over the Irfon and, on your LEFT, you will see a gate giving access to the riverside path. Go through this gate to walk with the water to your left (after having visited the village, if you wish). Go through a metal gate beside a disused kissing gate and carry on ahead. Pass through another metal gate, cross a tiny footbridge to reach another gate, which you go through and continue. The river narrows slightly and tumbles over rocks as you reach another gate, which you pass through. Go through yet another gate and continue, crossing a footbridge and passing through another gate before veering right through woodland by the river. The Lake Hotel can be seen up to your left as you pass through a gate to reach the road.

5 Turn LEFT to walk along the road, passing the Lake Hotel and Restaurant to your left and the Golf House. The road climbs quite steeply, passing a small golf course to the left. When the road swings to the left, cross a stile on the left and continue diagonally across a field: when you reach a fence corner continue beyond this, following a straggly line of trees (the remains of a hedge) to turn LEFT through what was once a gateway and then, after enjoying the fine view ahead, veer RIGHT to walk towards a gate to the left of houses. Go through the gate and go half LEFT to another gate before a farm.

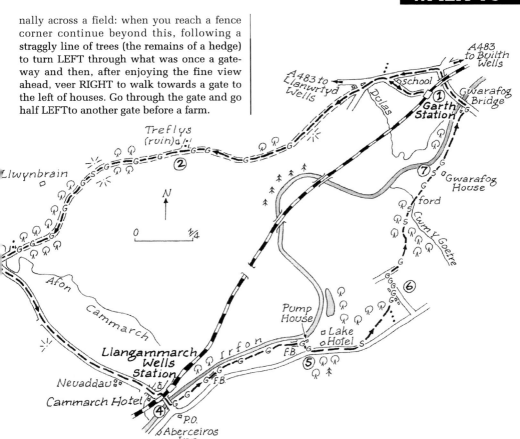

6 Go through this gate and turn LEFT, to enter a farmyard through a gate. Walk down the yard, with the farmhouse on your right, to leave it by a gate on the opposite side, and carry on ahead between sheds to reach two gates. Go through the RIGHT-hand gate to follow a track. Carry on ahead, keeping the fence to your left, until you reach a gate on the LEFT. Go through this and walk downhill, with the course of a stream to your left. As you enter sparse woods keep ahead, now with the course of a stream to your right. Follow the stream as it bends to the right and, when you reach a stile, cross it and continue ahead, keeping Cwm y Goetre to your right. A waymark on a tree confirms your route. You descend to stile, which you

cross and continue ahead, to carefully ford the stream, picking your way where the water is shallow. Carry on, with the stream swinging away and leaving to your left. Go through a gateway on your left and continue ahead, with the fence to your right.

7 Do not go right by Gwarafog House, but continue ahead to go through a gate into a wood with the river to your left. The path rises up and you continue along the field's edge to join the road through a gateway to the right of a white wooden house and turn LEFT. Cross the bridge, walk under the railway bridge to reach the main road, where you turn LEFT. Continue along the road, soon turning LEFT to return to the station.

27

WALK 14

A VISIT TO ST DAVID'S

DESCRIPTION This is an interesting 5½ mile walk with great views. The walk initially follows the valley floor and continues alongside the Afon Irfon passing below the kite feeding area and Victoria Wells towards Llanwrtyd Church. It then climbs steadily, after a short section of road walking, into the forest. You then turn abruptly to exit this to walk down by the side of the Nant Cerdin. As you climb above the Nant Cerdin there are some lovely views of the rolling countryside. **Do not attempt this walk after heavy rain, as the route involves fording the Nant Cerdin.** Allow 3 hours
START Llanwrtyd Wells SN883464.

I Leave the station, and turn left along Station Road. When this joins Irfon Terrace, maintain your direction to reach the town centre. Cross the main road by the Neuadd Arms and walk along Dolecoed Road: Tourist Information is available at the Neuadd Arms. Turn left and walk on the river side by the old Dol-y-Coed Hotel, now an electronics company. *This was formally a farmhouse prominent in the development of the spa trade.* Continue through a gate at the upstream end of the hotel and turn left down a path and through a gate. Ignore the track ahead. Follow the path on the bank of the Irfon to cross a footbridge that has a gate at the start and finish. At the far side turn right and follow the track as it veers left away from the river into a field. Go half left across this to a gate in the top corner. Go through this and follow the path up to join the road opposite the entrance to the Victoria Wells Log Cabin Motel. Turn right down the road and follow it until the tarmac ends. Go straight ahead. Climb over a stile left of a gate and follow a grassy track keeping to the right of conifers to a stile right of a gate. Climb over the stile and curve leftwards to climb over another stile to join a track. Turn right and follow this track that becomes a tarmac road leading back to Llanwrtyd.

2 Turn right in front of the church and cross the bridge over the Afon Irfon. *The Church of St David's is a pretty building standing in a fine situation, built on the site of an earlier church founded by St David around 530 AD. Wales' most celebrated composer of hymns, William Williams, was curate here from 1740-43, and his portrait hangs on the south wall. His grave can be visited at St Mary's, near Llandovery. A Celtic cross, which can be seen near the font, may date from the founding of the church. In winter the building is warmed by a stove manufactured by Gurney's Warming & Ventilating Co.* Continue along the road until just past a row of terraced cottages. Turn sharp left – signed to Alltwineu. Continue up this narrow road to a 'Y' junction. Go left (right goes to Kilsby) through a gate. Continue up the narrow road and go right at the next fork. Walk over a cattle grid continuing up the narrow steep road and through a gate. Continue up to two more. Pass through the right hand one indicated by a waymark, and follow the rough track to where it ends close to a finger post. Continue straight ahead on a path and enter the forest through a gate.

3 Follow the track as it descends to a main forest road. Cross over this slightly leftwards and walk down a narrow track. Cross a stream and follow the track up to where it levels. Keep walking ahead until a short steep descent leads to the Nant Cerin. Cross this. In high water this may be impassable. Turn right immediately after crossing and follow the path that often doubles for a stream! Pass to the right of a marker post and keep following the path to join a track. Turn right and follow it, ignoring a fork to the left. Walk along to where a track goes right. Continue straight ahead over a cattle grid. Follow the level track to the next cattle grid.

4 Turn right just before this and go up an indistinct path to an isolated bridle gate. Pass this to the left and follow a steep grassy path trending left up the hill to join a fence. Keep this to your left and continue up the hill passing a gate in the fence on your left. Continue ahead still with the fence to your

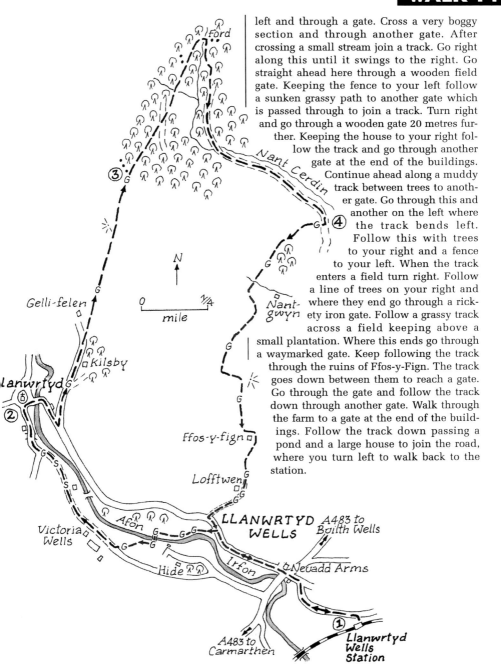

left and through a gate. Cross a very boggy section and through another gate. After crossing a small stream join a track. Go right along this until it swings to the right. Go straight ahead here through a wooden field gate. Keeping the fence to your left follow a sunken grassy path to another gate which is passed through to join a track. Turn right and go through a wooden gate 20 metres further. Keeping the house to your right follow the track and go through another gate at the end of the buildings. Continue ahead along a muddy track between trees to another gate. Go through this and another on the left where the track bends left. Follow this with trees to your right and a fence to your left. When the track enters a field turn right. Follow a line of trees on your right and where they end go through a rickety iron gate. Follow a grassy track across a field keeping above a small plantation. Where this ends go through a waymarked gate. Keep following the track through the ruins of Ffos-y-Fign. The track goes down between them to reach a gate. Go through the gate and follow the track down through another gate. Walk through the farm to a gate at the end of the buildings. Follow the track down passing a pond and a large house to join the road, where you turn left to walk back to the station.

LAND OF MINERALS

DESCRIPTION The Cambrian Mountains offer some of the wildest walking in Wales. This challenging 7 mile walk leads through wetlands and moors to Rhandirmwyn, nestled in the beautifully wooded Tywi Valley, then returning to Cynghordy, and its finely constructed railway viaduct. Allow about 4 hours.

START Cynghordy Station. SN802406.

1 Leave the lonely platform of Cynghordy halt by way of the access track but turn RIGHT at the first junction to the level crossing. Climb over the stile and listen for trains. If all is clear cross over and climb a stile into a field to follow the track up to a stile by a gate. Continue ahead as the track bends right to Dildre to the left of a huge shed, and through a gate. Walk up and across the field to the left of a line of trees. Continue through a gateway. Interesting this, there is no gate and the right gate post has a fence attached to it but not to the left! Walk down the field half LEFT to a gate. Go through it and down a track for 20 yards into wet ground. Turn sharp LEFT to pass through a very rickety iron gate. Go ahead for 10 yards then turn RIGHT and cross a small footbridge into a field. Walk up the field with a fence on the right to a stile at the top corner.

2 Go LEFT to cross a track and continue up to a stile by a gate. Cross it and continue through a wet pasture to a bridle gate. Go through and keep ahead with a fence on the left. Pass through a bridle gate by a dwelling known as Tascon. Proceed ahead again with a fence on the left to pass through a barred gate. The fence cuts left but keep ahead across marshy ground to go through a bridle gate. *The view back to the Brecon Beacons is superb.* Turn RIGHT and walk with the hedge on the RIGHT but go half LEFT through more wet ground to reach two gateways as indicated by a waymark on a tree. Go through the one on the left and continue ahead with a fence and trees on

the right. It descends more steeply to a track. Turn RIGHT and follow the track to a gate before a farm. Go through it and continue ahead between the house on the left and outbuildings on the right to exit over bridge and through a gate. Follow the track up the hillside to a gate and a road.

3 Cross the road and turn RIGHT to go through a gate into a field. Continue to rise up the field with a hedge on the left. Go through a gate at the next boundary and follow a green track with a fence on the right but ignoring a gate on the right. There's a cairn on the summit to your left and then a gate facing a mountain of conifers ahead. Go through it and follow it to a gate into the wood. Follow this between the trees and a fence. Ignore the gate on the right but rise up to a junction. Go LEFT to descend on a wide track for about half a mile. Pass over a stream in a narrow gully and then look for a stone cairn on the left.

4 Go LEFT at the cairn on a well worn path beneath conifers. This drops down to a gateway. Continue ahead to leave the wood to join a track. Turn RIGHT and go through a gate onto the road. Pass by the Royal Oak Inn, turn LEFT and first RIGHT at the junction on the road through Rhandirmwyn. *The area has been subject to mining for lead and zinc and the last mine was closed in the early 1930s hence its name meaning 'land containing minerals' in Welsh. The Royal Oak is a stone flagged inn with real character, serving great ale and food with a warm welcome. It is open at lunchtimes (to 15.00 in the summer, 14.00 in the Winter) and from 18.00 in the evening (19.00 on Sunday). It also has accommodation which is ideal for those seeking to explore the Upper Towy Valley (theroyaloakinn.co.uk). There's also a tearoom and store at the T junction.*

5 Turn LEFT by St Barnabus church to follow a track to a sewage works. Cross a stile by a gate and go ahead through a bridle gate to join a riverside path. Turn LEFT to follow this beautiful waterside path (Towy Trail) over a footbridge. Ignore the stile on

woodland. At the next junction, go LEFT and cross a stile, track and another stile. Continue up the hillside and at the next junction go LEFT to cross a stile then RIGHT on a byway a few yards beyond which climbs the hillside. This veers RIGHT to go through a gate on to a road.

6 Cross the road to walk up a narrow lane signposted to Llanerchindda. As the lane bends sharply LEFT keep ahead through a gate on a byway. At the junction go RIGHT through a gate and follow the track, a very wet one, through two more gates to a dwelling at Pendrainllwyn. Pass between the house and outbuildings to go through a gate onto a road. Turn LEFT and follow this down to Cynghordy, passing beneath the railway in a magnificent tunnel. At the junction, go LEFT as signposted to the railway station and LEFT again along a track. Turn RIGHT for the station platform.

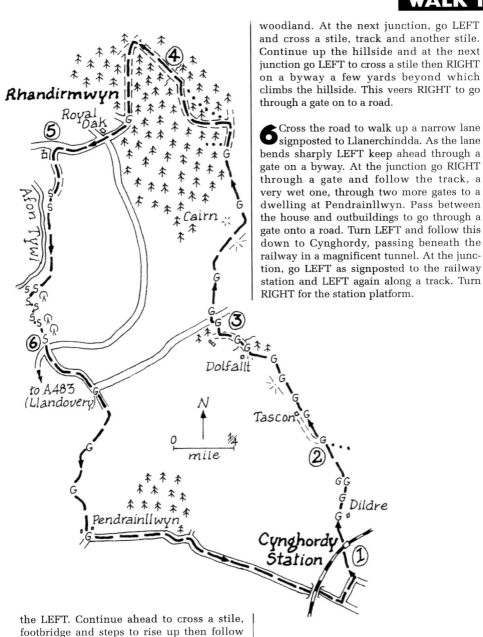

the LEFT. Continue ahead to cross a stile, footbridge and steps to rise up then follow a fence on the LEFT to the next stile. Cross it and proceed ahead (not RIGHT) on a permissive path to cross a stile by a gate. Cross it and go LEFT at the fork to rise through

A WALK IN 'WILD WALES'

DESCRIPTION George Borrow, author, traveller and charming eccentric, wrote his book 'Wild Wales' in 1854, recording a journey he made, on foot, through Wales. This moderate 3 mile walk visits the Castle Inn, Llandovery, where he stayed, and gives you a taste of the journey he made, as well as a splendid stroll beside the Tywi. The very many kissing gates make this an ideal walk for loved ones as the gates only open after kisses are made (!) Allow 2 kisses per gate! and about 1½ hours for the walk.
START Llandovery SN763345.

From the station go RIGHT to walk into the town centre, turning left to pass the Castle Hotel. *The great traveller George Borrow stayed on his journey through Wales on the 9th November 1854. He recounted the story of his journey in the very readable 'Wild Wales'.* Continue along the main road passing the Tourist Information Centre to reach the road bridge spanning the Afon Bran. Beforehand turn left along a path by the side of the terraced houses. Continue along the narrow tarmac path, with the houses to your left, to a kissing gate at its end. Bear right along the track with the river on your right to a path going off to the left below the next gate. DO NOT go through the gate. Follow the path with houses to your left and fence to your right. At a stile on your right turn left – do not go over the stile – to reach a road. Turn right and follow it to a marker post. Follow the path to the right and walk to a small gateway. Walk through this and pass to the right of a play area. Keep on this tarmac path to another gate. Go through this to join the A483.

2 Carefully cross the busy road and follow the minor road quite steeply uphill to St. Mary's Church. Opposite the church on the other side of the road is a stile and a marker post. Cross the stile and head straight down the field to a hedge on your left. Continue to cross another stile and a further one 20 yards ahead. Walk up steps to the railway line. Cross over making sure there are no trains and walk down steps on the far side to a stile. Climb over this and go slightly left to another, easily seen across the pasture. Cross over and continue walking straight ahead and away from a tiny stream on your left to yet another stile. Go over this and turn right to a gate. DO NOT go through this but walk down to your left for 10 yards to a waymarked stile.

3 Step over the stile and follow the path alongside the stream on your left. Cross three short sections of boardwalk. Keep following the stream and fence to a footbridge, where there is a waymark. Cross this and go over a stile to your left. Cross another footbridge 30 yards further on. Turn right, keeping the trees to your right, along the edge of the field towards a stile to the left of a gate. Cross the stile. Go left with a fence and trees to your left and walk up to a marker post. Follow the track, ignoring the one going down to the left. Keep walking along the track to a stile by a waymarked gate. Cross this and walk down the track for 50 yards to cross a stile on your left. Walk down the grassy path to yet another stile. Go over this to join a farm track. Go straight across this and go over another waymarked stile to join a tarmac road. Turn left then almost immediately right. Walk up to Pont Dolauhirion.

4 Do not walk over the bridge but turn down left to cross a stile. Follow the bank of the Afon Tywi through 3 kissing gates. After passing through the third gate, situated above small rapids, follow the edge of the field round to another kissing gate on your right. Go through this and walk up a narrow path to the left of a stream. The path ends at a kissing gate by a narrow road, and the stone bridge with a wooden footbridge immediately beyond. Cross the footbridge and pass through another kissing gate. Keep to the edge of the field, with a hedge on your right at first then a stone wall to, yes, another kissing gate. Go through this to join a narrow tarmac road. Cross straight over to go through another kissing gate. Go ahead along the edge of the field with a fence and farm buildings to your right to the familiar sight of a kissing gate. Pass through this too and bearing right will lead you to a corrugated iron shed. Go through another kissing gate to the right of the shed and continue walking between fences to a stile by a gate. Climb over the stile and ignoring the gates to your left continue straight ahead passing through two more kissing gates. After the second one follow the path between the hedge on your left and a fence to your right to a final kiss at the last kissing gate. Go through to join the A40 and turn left back to the station and a cup of tea in the tea room.

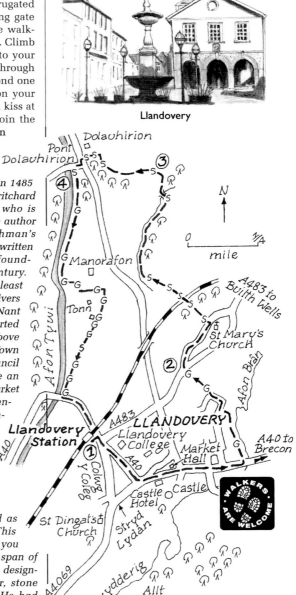

Llandovery

*L*andovery *is a medieval town and borough receiving its charter in 1485 from Richard III. The famous Rhys Pritchard 1579–1644 was vicar of Llandovery who is particularly remembered for being the author of 'Ganwyll y Cymry' – The Welshman's Candle – a popular devotional work written in Welsh. Llandovery College was founded in the early part of the 19th century. Llandovery takes its name from the least worthy and very insignificant of the rivers that surround the town. Called the Nant Bawddwr – dirty water – it was diverted in 1836 through an arched culvert above which the street above paved. The Town Hall was built in 1858. The actual council Chamber was situated directly above an open arcaded market. The former Market Hall, built in the 1840s, has been renovated and now houses a craft centre atop of which is the town clock. At one time there was a tradition of clock making in the town. Information on the Castle can be found on the information board below it in the car park.*

*P*ont Dolauhirion *was mentioned as the 'Bridge at Dolhir' in 1396. This was a timber structure and the bridge you see today was built in 1773. It has a span of 30 yards and cost £800 to build. The designer was William Edwards, a minister, stone mason and a self-taught architect. He had become world famous for the bridge he had built at Pontypridd in 1750.*

33

THE TWO CASTLES WALK

DESCRIPTION This short and easy 4 mile walk from Llandeilo will introduce you to the delights of both the Old and New Dinefwr Castle. The walk will take about 2½ hours, but you must add plenty of visiting time.
START Llandeilo SN633226.

Leave Llandeilo Station by walking up the steps and following the brick-laid path. When you reach the road, turn LEFT and walk gently uphill along Heol Alan. You arrive at the main road, where you turn LEFT to walk into the town. Ignore the sign indicating Parc Dinefwr to your right, and carry on along the main street. Just by the zebra crossing you reach an alleyway on the left leading to The White Horse, the home of Evan Evans Brewery and a good stop for refreshment. Continue along the main street, passing St Teilo's Church to your left. Continue down the hill, keeping to the right-hand side of the road. Turn RIGHT before the bridge and walk with the Afon Tywi on your left.

2 You come to two gates side by side. Go through the kissing gate on the RIGHT and follow the track. *Castle Woods encompass 60 acres of ancient woodland, where you should look out for great, lesser spotted, and green woodpecker, tree creeper, goldcrest, jay, magpie, sparrow-hawk, peregrine falcon, tawny owl, pied flycatcher, and redstart.* When the path forks by a noticeboard, go LEFT to reach the church. Follow the path around the church and go down to a gate. Go through this and turn up to your right for 10 yards to another gate, and go through. You are now on National Trust property. Walk beside the fence on your left. Go through a gate, which is shortly followed by another gate to your left. Go through and follow the path uphill through woodland. Go through a kissing gate and walk along a track, with the fence to your left. When you reach a kissing gate on your LEFT, go

through and follow the path into the woods. Eventually you reach a junction with a prominent track, where you turn LEFT. You now climb steadily up to Old Dinefwr Castle. *Used as a hill fort by the Romans, the first recorded mention of this castle is in the Book of Llandaff, which refers to the site in the 7thC. It was almost certainly built around 850 AD by Rhodri Fawr in response to Viking incursions. On his death Rhodri split Wales into three kingdoms. The southern kingdom, Deheubarth, was controlled from here. By 950 Hywel Dda, Wales' most renowned leader, was based here, and Dinefwr flourished at this time. But when the Normans continued their invasion into Wales in 1067, Dinefwr's influence waned, until Rhys ap Gruffydd, new Lord of Dinefwr, began his struggle for Welsh independence in 1135, upon the death of Henry I. With others he regained independence, along with most of the land lost to the Normans. It is worth noting that Rhys was a great patron of the arts, who staged the first National Eisteddfod at Cardigan Castle in 1176. Upon his death in 1197 his sons struggled for his lands, and eventually Rhys Grug emerged with the controlling hand. He burnt the town of Swansea, took control of other castles and was eventually killed, fittingly it seems, in battle. The great Welsh Prince Llewelyn ap Iorwerth then came to power, and turned his attentions to Dinefwr. Following Llewelyn's death in 1240 there followed various changes in ownership until, in 1277, Edward I began his march into Wales, and captured Dinefwr. It was never to be returned to the Welsh. It withstood Owain Glyndwr's rebellion in 1403, and was finally abandoned by the Rhys family around 1600. The Summer House, or Belvedere, was built on top of the keep in 1660. The castle has only fairly recently been restored, and is now open. Entry charge for both properties.*

3 When you have explored the castle, return along the path, passing the junction then turning left to a bridle-gate below a red-roofed house. Go through, following a lane beneath a red-roofed house. Go through the gate ahead and continue along the lane. Cross a cattle grid to reach the National Trust Information Centre and Shop, *where*

you can purchase tickets to visit the entire site, and watch a short introductory video. Access is gained just beyond the shop. Deriving its name from the new town established in the area by Edward I in 1298, New Dinefwr Castle or Newton House is thought to date from 1603, although there had been a 'Newton House' in these parts since about 1430. The present building was periodically altered and extended, and the grounds were inspected by the landscape architect Capability Brown in 1775, although his ideas were probably never executed. Used during the Second World War as a Casualty Clearing Station, the house, after being sold by Lord Dinefwr in the late 1970s, fell into disrepair, and was finally taken over by The National Trust in 1990. They have done their usual excellent work, restoring much of the building to its former state. The park contains a herd of fallow deer and rare white cattle, fine oaks and lakes. Many interesting minor out-buildings surround the house. Park & Castle open daily 10.00-18.00 (closes 16.00 in winter. Newton House opens at 11.00. Entrance charge for both properties.

4 Now leave the house by taking the main approach road – or if you wish you can walk around the edge of the park in front of the building – this path joins the approach road further down. Follow the main approach road and, when you reach a wooden gate on your RIGHT, go through to follow a shady path. When you reach a signpost indicating Llandyfeisant Church, turn LEFT to walk steeply uphill on a stepped path through woods. Go through a gate and continue AHEAD to reach the main road. Turn RIGHT to walk back into the town, passing the Old Market Hall on your left. Turn LEFT at the main road. Now continue until you reach Heol Alan, where you turn RIGHT to return to the station.

WALK 18

ONE FOR THE BIRDS

DESCRIPTION This easy 6½ mile walk between Pontarddulais and Bynea stations takes you over level ground beside the lower reaches of the Afon Llwchwr, once overshadowed by a steelworks and a colliery either side of the river at Bynea, but now splendid bird-watching country. Allow about 4 hours, wear waterproof footware, and bring your binoculars!

IMPORTANT NOTE The path beyond the M4 motorway bridge can become flooded at certain high tides, so please ensure that you check the time of high tide before embarking upon this walk. This information can be found in newspapers such as *The Western Mail*. BBC Wales also give high water times for the following day for the south-Wales coast at *approximately 18.50, Monday to Friday.*

START Pontarddulais SN588040 or Bynea SS550991.

1 From Pontarddulais Station walk to the main road and turn LEFT, and then ahead at the crossroads. When the road forks, go RIGHT on the main street. When you reach the Farmers Arms on the right, turn RIGHT, and then fork LEFT along Coed Bach. At the end of the road enter Coed Bach Park, and take the main path, to the right. When the path bends to the right, carry on ahead, along a grassy bank between two football pitches to reach a path. Follow this to the right and then left, around the wire fence of the rugby pitch. The path crosses the now dismantled line of an old railway track through a kissing gate.

2 Go through a kissinggate (on the right) and walk ahead to another kissing gate. Follow the path to the riverside and go LEFT. Cross the footbridge and kissing gate and continue through reeds. Go through two kissing gates, cross a footbridge and then, with a fence on youir right, proceed throughj two kissing gates towards towards a farm. Go through the gate and go left along the track towards the motorway.

3 You pass under the motorway, then cross a stile and follow the track as it at first bends to the left, and then to the right. Walk under the railway and continue ahead. Cross the bridge over the stream by Castell-du, turn RIGHT and climb a stile. Follow the distinct track, which bends to the left and becomes a path, with the estuary over to the right. Cross a stile and continue ahead, crossing a stream by a footbridge and track to negotiate another stile, and then walk with the fence on your right. When the fence curves away to the right, continue ahead over a boggy patch to arrive at a stile. Cross it and carry on ahead. *The Llwchwr Estuary is a splendid place to watch birds, although you will certainly see a far greater variety during the autumn and winter. During the summer you should watch out for greenshank, which nest in north-west Scotland but move south during late summer to feed around the estuary, and little egrets, which can often be seen under the arches of the bridges: they winter south of the Mediterranean. During autumn and winter the estuary comes into its own, supporting large numbers of shelduck, widgeon, teal, mallard, oyster catcher and lapwing.* Carefully climb another stone step stile, which can be well hidden during the summer and continue veering slightly left to a second stone stile. Cross this and continue ahead. Negotiate another stone stile, and continue ahead to a wooden stile. Climb it, cross a bridge and go LEFT on the lane for 10 yards then go RIGHT through a gate.

4 Keep ahead with a hedge on the right to veer right and walk through marshy ground to the top corner of the field to reach a stile. Cross it and the bridge and turn LEFT, to walk with a hedge on your left. *There are clumps of scarlet pimpernel and iris here in season.* You reach a kissing gate on the left. Go through it and then veer to the right. When you reach a stile by a gate, cross it and walk with a hedge on the right. When you come to a kissing-gate beyond a track, go through it and continue ahead to another stile beside a field gate. Continue, with a fence to the right, to a stile in the corner, 5 yards to the right of a field gate. Go LEFT then RIGHT to walk along the track. Go over a stile beside a gate by a house to reach a lane, which you cross.

5 Go through a kissing gate opposite and continue, veering a little to the left, to reach a kissing gate. Go through this and continue ahead with a hedge on the left. Reach a stile beside a fixed old wooden gate, cross it and carry on along the path. Cross astile and continue ahead to cross the subsequent stile. Now follow the track with a hedge to the right, crossing a stile by a gate to the track and go to the left.

6 Go through the kissing gate and turn RIGHT along a lane. Follow this lane bythe clearly indicated Foreshore Car Park. Turn RIGHT here to enter the park. Follow the park road, turning RIGHT when you reach the decoratively arranged railway sleepers, to arrive at the edge of the estuary. Go LEFT along the path with the water and sands to your right. Leave the park

7 Cross the river via the road bridge beside the railway *viaduct. This was built entirely of timber, by Isambard Kingdom Brunel, in 1852.* At the far end of the road bridge, turn RIGHT, descending steps, and continue ahead towards the INA Bearing Company. Turn LEFT at the end of the road, and continue, passing The Lewis Arms on your right. As you approach the main road, turn RIGHT and continue to reach Bynea Railway Station, to catch the train back. *Bynea Station once stood beside sidings which served the Bynea Steel Works and the Yspitty Tin Works.*

through a gate, passing a small group of factory buildings on your right. Continue along the road, to emerge by the bridge.

SHOVELERS & SNIPES

DESCRIPTION This walk follows the Wales Coastal Path from Bynea to Llanelli by way of the Wildfowl & Wetlands Trust (WWT) National Wetland Centre, and with superb views across to the Gower Peninsula. It is ideal for families with buggies or wheelchair users as there are no hills nor stiles. 6 miles, allow 3 hours.

START Bynea Station SS550992 or Llanelli Station SS506994.

1 From Bynea station walk up from either platform to Heol-y-Bwlch. Turn LEFT, cross the road and continue towards Loughor. Pass a garage on the right then Look for a concrete track on the right between buildings and a security fence. Go RIGHT along this track.

2 At the junction keep ahead (signposted Route 4) and then first RIGHT to walk over the suspension bridge. Continue on the wide track which descends to run alongside the Loughor estuary (shared with cyclists on the Celtic Trail). *Over ten miles of coastline has been developed as a the Coastal Millennium Park and this is an exceptional traffic free area through to Pembrey. There are great views across the estuary to Pen-clawdd and the Gower Peninsula. This also happens to be a section of the Wales Coastal Path and leads, in about one mile, to a road and entrance to the National Wetlands Centre of Wales on the left.*

*T**he Wildfowl and Wetlands Trust** have worked with others to develop a 450 acre site of lagoons, salt marches and streams which provide ideal habitats for a wide range of birds and mammals. There are regular sightings of birds from the shoveler to the snipe ,black tailed godwits and gadwells as well as a richness in plant and other animal*

life. The WWT National Wetlands Centre for Wales is open daily from 09.30 until 17.00; there's an entrance charge and during the autumn this includes a daily guided walk at 13.00 hours to check out migrating birds, fungi, and so on, so allow plenty of time to make the best of the midday walk here.

3 If you are not visiting then cross the road and continue ahead. Before reaching another road go LEFT (signposted Route 4 again) and follow the track as it bends left then right to skirt a golf course. There are several parallel paths looping off the main track if you prefer these, perhaps to get a closer view of the birdlife in the salt marshes. The track eventually comes to urban development at Machynys, turns RIGHT and joins a road alongside housing. *The old working villages associated with the tinplate and other works, the remains of which have now almost entirely gone. The area is being rebuilt with houses overlooking the sea; people who lived here 150 years ago would not*

Discovery Centre

Llanelli Station

LLANELLI

Machynys

Golf Course

recognise it now but there remains a strong interest in Llanelli's industrial heritage. Look out for the interpretation boards near to the route. It then cuts RIGHT again before an inlet to a path by a road bridge. Go LEFT to cross a bridge and the track continues towards the North Dock where the Coastal Park Discovery Centre is situated. Simply follow the trail to reach it.

4 However, if you are not going to call into the Discovery Centre, cross the road on the right before the roundabout and then keep RIGHT to walk into Stryd y Mor (Marine Road). Follow this until you reach

Glanmor Road easily identified by two historic chapels located nearby. *The Bethel Baptist Chapel and the Siolah Independent Chapels both date from1840 but the former was enlarged in 1850. Llanelli, like many of the rapidly expanding industrial areas of South Wales has a large number of on-conformist chapels from this period which have served the local population since then but also give character to many local neighbourhoods.* Go LEFT along it to the crossing gates. Once across turn RIGHT into Great Western Crescent and the entrance to Llanelli station on the rght.

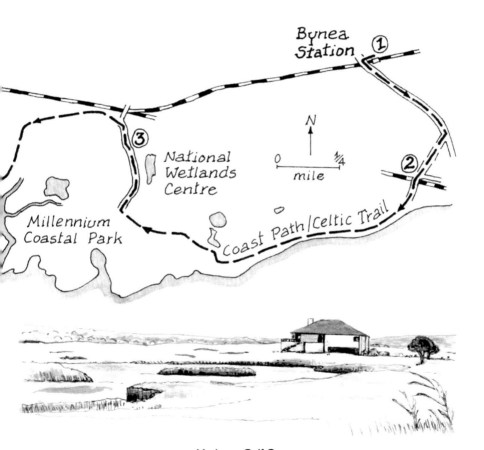

Machynys Golf Course

WALK 20

'A WORLD WITHIN A WORLD OF THE SEA TOWN'

DESCRIPTION 'An ugly, lovely town (or so it was, and is, to me) crawling, sprawling, slummed, unplanned, jerry-villa'd and smug-suburbed by the side of a long and splendid-curving shore where truant boys and sandfield boys and old anonymous men, in the tatters and hangovers of a hundred charity suits, beach combed, idled, and paddled, watched the dock-bound boats, threw stones into the sea for the barking outcast dogs, and, on Saturday summer afternoons, listened to the militant music of salvation and hell-fire preached from a soap-box'... This was the Swansea of the inimitable poet and playwright Dylan Thomas, the city's most famous son. He was born in 'a Glamorgan villa' in Cwmdonkin Road (visited on this route), and his memory is celebrated in the new centre down by the sea. Today this university city exudes a cosmopolitan air, typified by the extensive marina development explored on this walk. Swansea's latter-day wealth was built upon anthracite and iron ore, but only traces of this industry now remain. This easy walk is about 5 miles long and should take about 3 hours. There are plenty of opportunities to stop, to visit the sights, explore and take refreshment, so be sure to add on the time taken for this.

START Swansea SS657936.

Leave Swansea Railway Station and walk to the left along the High Street. You reach the ruins of Swansea Castle on the left. Now turn RIGHT into Castle Square. *The water sculpture here reflects upon Dylan Thomas' lines:*

'We sail a boat upon the path, paddle with leaves down an ecstatic line of light'
Dylan Marlais Thomas' (1914-53) unusual middle name derives from the celebrated radical Welsh poet William Thomas, brother of Dylan's paternal grandfather, who wrote as Gwilym Marles. Dylan Thomas married Caitlin in 1937, and later they lived in
Laugharne for a while. Now take the first LEFT into Princess Way. Now continue along Princess Way, and veer to the LEFT into York Street. You come to Victoria Road, which is usually busy with traffic. Cross carefully – there is a central reservation – to reach Cambrian Place and the Swansea Museum. *This museum is Wales' oldest, and still manages to delight visitors with its Egyptian mummy, Swansea and Nantgarw pottery and porcelain, 2000 years of local archaeology, a Victorian gallery and much more. Open 10.00-17.00 Tue-Sun & B. Hols.*

2 When you leave the museum turn RIGHT, then take the first LEFT into Adelaide Road, and walk to the end, where you turn RIGHT into Somerset Place. *On the left you will see The Dylan Thomas Centre, a fitting tribute to Swansea's most famous son. During July and August each year the Dylan Thomas Festival is centred here. Open 10.00-16.30 daily. There are also special events and performances.* Now turn RIGHT into East Burrows Road and walk to the end, where you turn RIGHT by Pocketts Wharf to continue along Manheim Quay, with the Tawe Basin on your left. *You pass the Pump House on your left, now converted into a pub, and the Dylan Thomas Theatre, with its splendid mural, on the right. On the waterfront, in front of the Pump House, there is a fine seated statue of Dylan Thomas.* Now continue along Victoria Quay, with the National Waterfront Museum *(open daily 10.00-17.00)* ahead and to your right, and some fine preserved craft moored to your left.

3 Walk along Victoria Quay with its bars and cafés, keeping the marina to your left, and turning LEFT at the end onto Arethusa Quay. Continue ahead, cross the road and go up steps by a building towards the sea front. Now turn RIGHT and walk along the seafront, or on the sands if you wish. Continue beside Oystermouth Road, or along the sands, until you reach the stone supports of a footbridge. Cross the road here and go LEFT to turn RIGHT along Gorse Lane, between the Patti Pavilion and St Helen's Cricket & Rugby Ground.

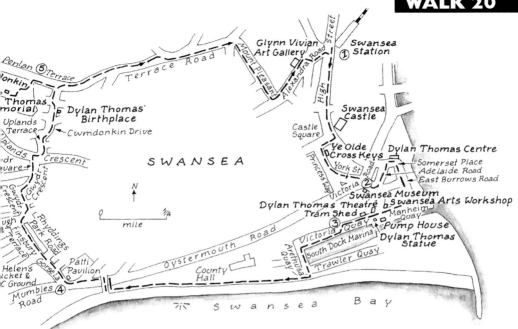

4 Continue ahead, passing the Cricketers pub, to walk up Finsbury Terrace. At the end of this road, turn RIGHT into Marlborough Road, then LEFT into Rhyddings Park Road. Walk ahead into Gwydr Crescent and follow this to the right to Gwydr Square and traffic lights at Uplands Crescent. Turn RIGHT, then very soon LEFT into Uplands Terrace. Walk to the top, and turn RIGHT. After a few yards you will find yourself in Cwmdonkin Drive. *Dylan Thomas' birthplace, at number 5, is near the top, on the right-hand side. It is remarkable only by its association with the great man.* Continue to the end of the road and turn LEFT into Penlan Terrace. Walk along here until you reach an entrance to Cwmdonkin Park on the left. Follow the paths downhill to explore it. *Cwmdonkin Park, built in 1874, was a childhood haunt of Dylan Thomas: 'Though it was only a little park, it held within its borders of old tall trees ... many secret places, caverns and forests, prairies and deserts, as a country somewhere at the end of the sea'. A fenced area encloses the Dylan Thomas Memorial Garden.*

5 Now leave the park the way you came in, and walk back along Penlan Crescent, with fine views of the harbour and the bay ahead and to your right. Pass through a pedestrian barrier in a narrow part of the road and continue ahead. You are now in Terrace Road. Continue ahead along Mount Pleasant. Pass Swansea Institute on your left. When you descend to the main road, turn LEFT. Soon you reach Alexandra Road, with the Glynn Vivian Art Gallery on the left. *Glynn Vivian was the fourth son of John Henry Vivian, owner of the largest copper works in Swansea. The collection is suitably eclectic, with paintings and prints merged with Toby jugs and glass paperweights. There are European and Oriental ceramics, and some fine grandfather clocks. The small garden contains sculpture, and there are visiting exhibitions. Open 10.00-17.00 Tue-Sun & B. Hols.* Now continue along Alexandra Road to return to Swansea Railway Station.

Extracts from *Reminiscences of Childhood, Rain Cuts the Place We Tread* and *Fern Hill*, all by Dylan Thomas, are reproduced by kind permission of the publisher, Dent.

Summary of the Walks

Walk number	Starting station	Grid ref of start	Length of walk (miles)	Grade (see below)	Average time to allow for one-way walk	Attractions
1	**Shrewsbury**	SO495128	3	E	2 hrs	Town trail
2	**Church Stretton**	SO456936	2½	E	2 hrs	Town and valley
3	**Craven Arms** or **Church Stretton**	SN432830 SO445935	8½	E	5 hrs	Pleasant countryside, Acton Scott Farm Museum [P]
4	**Craven Arms**	SN432830	5½	M	3½ hrs	Manor house, woods, church, earthworks, views [P]
5	**Hopton Heath** or **Broome**	SO380774 SO399809	6½	M	4 hrs	Pretty villages, river, churches [P]
6	**Hopton Heath** or **Bucknell**	SO776380 SO736356	5½	M	3½ hrs	Hopton Castle, woodland
7	**Bucknell** or **Knighton**	SO035736 SO292724	5	M	3 hrs	Church, Offa's Dyke Centre
8	**Knucklas** or **Llangunllo**	SO254741 SO210730	5	M	3 hrs	Viaduct, castle, church, pretty countryside [P]
9	**Llangunllo** or **Llanbister Road**	SO210730 SO174716	5 (8)	M	3 hrs 4½ hrs	Glyndŵr's Way, uplands, expansive views
10	**Llanbister Road** or **Dolau**	SO174716 SO140671	6½	E	3½ hrs	Coxhead Bank Common, castle mound
11	**Llandrindod Wells**	SO059613	7	M	4 hrs	Lake, church, castle [P]
12	**Cilmeri**	SO003512	8½	E	5 hrs	Church, River Wye, Llywelyn Memorial [P]
13	**Garth** or **Llangammarch**	SN954495 SN936473	6	M	3 hrs	Views, church, riverside, village [P]
14	**Llanwrtyd Wells**	SN883464	5½	E	3 hrs	Red kites, spa, church [P]
15	**Cynghordy**	SN802406	7	S	4 hrs	Wild moorland, River Tywi
16	**Llandovery**	SN763345	3	M	1½ hrs	George Borrow's 'Wild Wales' River Tywi [P]
17	**Llandeilo**	SO633226	4	E	2½ hrs	Two castles, views, park, [P]
18	**Pontarddulais** or **Bynea**	SN588040 SS550991	6½	E	4 hrs	Estuary, birds, bridges [P]
19	**Bynea** or **Llanelli**	SS550992 SS506994	6	E	3 hrs	WWT centre, heritage
20	**Swansea**	SS657936	5	E	3 hrs	Dylan Thomas sights, harbour, seashore, gallery [P]

Walk grading — This is for guidance only.

E	**Easy**	Any uphill sections are short and not steep
M	**Moderate**	Involves some uphill walking, but easily managed by a reasonably fit person
S	**Strenuous**	Several climbs and rough ground requiring a good level of fitness
[P]		Pub en route

The Heart of Wales Line

If **you are travelling** along this line for the first time, you will be impressed. Seasoned travellers will need no reminding of the rugged beauty, tranquil villages and picturesque Victorian spa towns that are dotted along one of the most scenic lines in the United Kingdom.

For 121 miles between Shrewsbury and Swansea a feast of panoramic views includes the remote borderlands of the English Marches, the Radnor Forest between Knighton and Llandrindod Wells, red kites in the skies above the Eppynt hills near Llanwrtyd Wells, the meandering River Tywi between Llandovery and Llandeilo, and the beautiful Loughor estuary near Llanelli.

The impressive viaducts at Knucklas and Cynghordy are two of the seven bridges crossed on a journey which also includes six tunnels, and rises to 980 feet above sea level.

The Heart of Wales Line Forum

is a consortium of local authorities, the railway industry, the Welsh Development Agency, tourism bodies and the Travellers Association, all committed to the retention and development of the Heart of Wales Railway Line.

KEY TO THE MAPS

- **→** Walk route and direction
- Metalled road
- --- Unsurfaced road
- •••• Footpath/route adjoining walk route
- ∿∿ River/stream
- 🌲 Trees
- ▬▬ Railway
- **G** Gate
- **S** Stile
- **F.B.** Footbridge
- Viewpoint
- **P** Parking

THE COUNTRY CODE

- Be safe – plan ahead and follow any signs
- Leave gates and property as you find them
- Protect plants and animals, and take your litter home
- Keep dogs under close control
- Consider other people

The CRoW Act 2000, implemented throughout Wales in May 2005, introduced new legal rights of access for walkers to designated open country, predominantly mountain, moor, heath or down, plus all registered common land. This access can be subject to restrictions and closure for land management or safety reasons for up to 28 days a year.

Published by
Kittiwake Books Limited 3 Glantwymyn Village Workshops, Machynlleth, Montgomeryshire SY20 8LY

© Text: Heart of Wales Line Forum 2013
© Maps: Kittiwake Books Limited 2013
© Drawings: Kittiwake-Books Limited 2013
Cover Pictures: *Main* – Knucklas Viaduct; *inset* – St Mary's Bucknell. *David Perrott*
First edition 2003. Revised edition 2011.
New enlarged edition 2013

Care has been taken to be accurate. However neither the author nor the publisher can accept responsibility for any errors which may appear, or their consequences. If you are in doubt about any access, or your ability to walk any of the paths shown, check before you proceed.
Some paths may be being upgraded, with kissing-gates often being used to replace stiles.

Printed by Mixam Print, UK.

ISBN: **978 1 908748 08 9**

THE HEART OF WALES LINE
'The little train with big horizons'

Linking the West Midlands with South West Wales, our line provides unbeatable access to the rural heart of Wales. *Here's a selection of places to explore:*

Shrewsbury: Medieval town, galleries, museum, great shops, park, theatre.

Church Stretton: 'Little Switzerland' – great local shops, walks up the Long Mynd

Craven Arms: for the Discovery Centre, and nearby Stokesay Castle

Knighton: 'the Town on Offa's Dyke' – mid way point on this famous trail and one end of Glyndŵr's Way National Trail

Knucklas: famous railway viaduct, 12th century hilltop castle remains and community gardens

Llandrindod Wells: Victorian spa town par excellence, museum with Roman display, National Cycle Museum, town architecture trail.

Builth Road: Royal Welsh Showground – hosts shows all year round; nearby Wyeside Arts Centre

Cilmeri: Commemorative stone for Llywellyn ap Grufydd, last native Prince of Wales, who was slain nearby

Llangammarch Wells: country house hotel, fishing

Llanwrtyd Wells: great places to eat and stay: fine collection of eccentric events and activities

Llandovery: historic cattle drovers town, newly restored station tearoom, pubs, castle

Llandeilo: attractive small town with good shops (chocolatier, frocks!), nearby Dinefwr Park (NT)

Llanelli: largest town in Carmarthenshire, Coastal Park, Wildfowl & Wetlands Centre, big indoor market, new cinema and theatre

Swansea: beaches, shops, indoor market, university, parks, cafés, great pubs and clubs, and 'The Gateway to Gower'.

Many towns and villages along the line also have interesting historic churches. Visit www.ctnw.co.uk for an interactive map showing which are open.